The Institute of Biology's
Studies in Biology no. 23

Investigation by Experiment

by O. V. S. Heath D.Sc., F.R.S., F.I.Biol.

Director, Agricultural Research Council Unit
of Flower Crop Physiology,
Emeritus Professor of Horticulture,
University of Reading

Edward Arnold (Publishers) Ltd

First published 1970

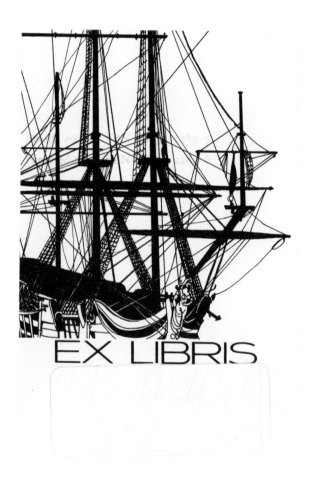

Printed in Great Britain by
William Clowes and Sons Ltd, London and Beccles

General Preface to the Series

It is no longer possible for one textbook to cover the whole field of Biology and to remain sufficiently up to date. At the same time students at school, and indeed those in their first year at universities, must be contemporary in their biological outlook and know where the most important developments are taking place.

The Biological Education Committee, set up jointly by the Royal Society and the Institute of Biology, is sponsoring, therefore, the production of a series of booklets dealing with limited biological topics in which recent progress has been most rapid and important.

A feature of the series is that the booklets indicate as clearly as possible the methods that have been employed in elucidating the problems with which they deal. Wherever appropriate there are suggestions for practical work for the student. To ensure that each booklet is kept up to date, comments and questions about the contents may be sent to the author or the Institute.

1970

INSTITUTE OF BIOLOGY
41 Queen's Gate
London, S.W.7

Preface

I have written this book in the belief that it is of the utmost importance that everyone should have some understanding of the nature, potentialities and limitations of science; also that we can only obtain this by carrying out original investigations ourselves. The methods of science are available to anyone for the solution of practical problems and the discovery of new knowledge in everyday life, but until this is generally realized and acted upon there will be little real understanding of science.

Experience of original scientific investigation should begin at school, and if a whole class or large group collaborates in each experiment, results of scientific value can be obtained in the short periods available. Biology is more suitable than Chemistry or Physics as some of its frontiers lie nearer.

It is possible to carry out and interpret scientific experiments with no mathematics except simple graphical methods and arithmetic, but mathematics and especially statistical methods provide most powerful tools. A good antidote to the fear of mathematics is a preliminary reading of SAWYER (1943), while a good elementary text on statistics such as BAILEY (1959) should be consulted as necessary; it must be emphasized that statistical methods are not likely to be understood without working through numerical examples.

Chapter one deals with basic ideas in rather general terms; in the rest of the book these are developed further with more attention to the mathematical ideas underlying them. It may be found useful to re-read Chapter one after finishing the whole book.

I hope that dogmatic statements, unavoidable in so short a book, will stimulate discussion rather than be accepted passively.

I am most grateful to Professor R. N. Curnow, Head of the Department of Applied Statistics, University of Reading, for reading the typescript and making many constructive criticisms. I of course take full responsibility for any errors that remain.

Reading   O.V.S.H.
1970

Contents

The Methods of Science   1

If we are going to attempt scientific investigation it is a good thing to give some thought to what science is and what are its methods. I suggest that science consists essentially in an attempt to understand the *relations* of selected aspects of things and events in the real world, an attempt which should have both intuitive and logical components, and which must be based on observation and tested by further observation. I shall not philosophize on how adequately our sensory experience reflects what is in the 'real' world, nor on what are things and events, but I do want to emphasize that science only deals with selected aspects of them. Science seeks always to classify and generalize, to make statements that will be true in the future of the relations of things and events of the same classes as those it has studied in the past. It may be assumed that no two things or events are exactly alike in every respect and therefore complete description, even if possible, would result in classes each consisting of a single unique individual that would never again recur. If, for instance, we were comparing the rates of growth of piebald rats on two diets, we might record their weights at suitable intervals and classify them as male or female and by age, but we should probably ignore the growth in length of their whiskers and the differences in their black and white patterns as well as a host of other attributes.

The reader may like to try making his own definition of science, but if mine is accepted it implies that mathematics is not a science and this I hold to be true. Mathematics consists of a number of systems of logic written in shorthand, which can be used to study relations by themselves without reference to things or events; unlike science it does not need observations (data) but only postulates, which need have no relevance to the real world. However, some branches of applied mathematics can be of the greatest importance in dealing with scientific data and scientific ideas; statistics is one of these. It must be realized that, as with a computer, what comes out depends on what goes in; if you make the wrong postulates mathematics provides you with answers which may well be mathematically correct but are not scientifically correct.

1.1   The methods of observational and theoretical science

STAGE 1. It begins, as all science must, with *observations* of things in the real world and what they do (events). In theoretical science the theoretician makes use of other people's observations. In what I have called observational science, the scientist, who might for instance be an astronomer or an ecologist, makes observations of his own. This observation and recording of selected aspects of things and events, without disturbing them more than is necessary in order to observe them, is natural history. Although not by itself science, natural history is essential, for it suggests the problems for science to attempt to solve. It has been said that 'one cannot cerebrate *in vacuo*', which might be paraphrased as 'if you don't know anything you can't think about it'.

OBSERVATIONAL SCIENCE

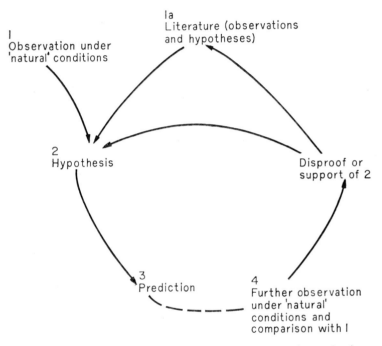

Fig. 1–1   Formal scheme for the processes of non-experimental science. For explanation see text.

STAGE 2. The next stage is to think of an explanation for some feature of the observations that has excited our interest. This explanation is called a *hypothesis*, or in plain language a guess, but if it is to avoid being pure fantasy it must be an informed guess—that is to say it should ideally be consistent with all the relevant observations that have been made, and should at least be consistent with all that we know about. If we publish our hypothesis people will then inform us of a lot of other observations with which it appears inconsistent and in this way it may be stifled soon after birth by existing knowledge. However, even if our first hypothesis does not deserve to live, there will remain a large number of other possible hypotheses which can apparently account for our set of observations. Out of those we can think of we must choose one, our choice depending on our imaginative capacity, our knowledge, our prejudices and habits of thought: this is where intuition comes in. At this stage, one hypothesis may be as good as another, your guess as good as mine, and in order to qualify as a part of science the hypothesis must be tested against new observations devised for that purpose.

Hypotheses are sometimes stated in the form of mathematical equations, or so-called mathematical models, and the theoretician, who enters the field at this stage, is especially apt to use these; although they help to avoid the ambiguity inherent in words they are not an *essential* part of science.

STAGE 3. We must next make a logical *prediction* of certain consequences of the hypothesis which, under specified natural conditions, should be observable if it is true, but which have not yet been observed. The theoretician then hands over again to the observational scientist who has to wait for the specified natural conditions to occur. This may take a very long time. For example, astronomers had to wait for a total eclipse of the sun to observe the bending of light in a gravitational field, as predicted by Einstein's general theory of relativity. If the ecologist were to make predictions as to the abundance of plants of species which colonize drying mud in Britain, such as *Limosella aquatica* (SALISBURY, 1967), he would have to wait for a drought. These long delays usually make it impossible to carry through an original investigation in observational science in the short times available to students at school or University.

STAGE 4. When the appropriate natural conditions occur, the *further observations* may disprove the hypothesis or fail to disprove it—they can never prove it, but if they agree with it they may be said to support it. When a hypothesis has received a good deal of support it achieves a measure of respectability and is called a theory, and when it has survived a very large number of observations it may even become a law; even so it is always open to disproof by some devastating new observation, just as the discovery of the bending of light in a gravitational field disproved the 'law' that light always travels in straight lines. Such disproof of a law usually leaves it still holding as a first approximation (for most purposes light does travel in straight lines) and it must be realized that science only deals in approximations which are successively improved as work proceeds. There is no such thing as an 'exact science' though some are more inexact than others.

If our hypothesis has been disproved we must think of a new one and go round again; if it has been supported we should wish to extend or improve it. In either case we may visit the library (Fig. 1–1, 1a) and take in contributions from the literature; the library is where the theoretician starts. Although the diagram suggests a circular process it should really be a helix, or perhaps a volute.

Note that in observational science comparisons are made between the initial observations (Fig. 1–1, 1) and others (Fig. 1–1, 4) made much later and often in a different place. This gives many opportunities for irrelevant changes of circumstances in addition to the circumstances chosen by the investigator. The method thus tends to be inaccurate or, as we shall say later, subject to large 'random errors'.

1.2   The methods of experimental science

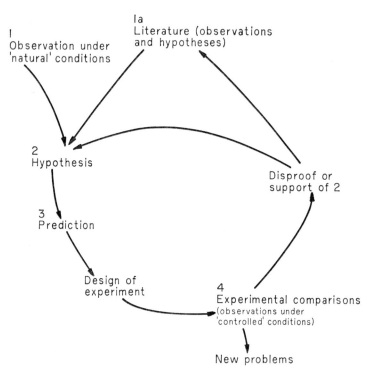

Fig. 1–2   Formal scheme for the processes of experimental science. For explanation see text.

Experimental science (Fig. 1–2) can be a faster moving and (to me) more exciting affair. Again, it should start with a problem raised by observation and again a hypothesis should be made to account for some feature or features of the observations, but instead of having to think of a prediction that can be tested by observation under natural conditions, we can now impose new conditions experimentally. This has three great advantages. First, we can design our experiment and, in many cases, carry it out without delay. Secondly, instead of the comparisons being between the widely separated stage 1 and stage 4 they are now all within stage 4, which becomes 'Experimental comparisons'. There is thus a gain of precision. Thirdly, the conditions or 'treatments' imposed can cover a much wider range than those provided by nature in observational science.

Often quite unexpected phenomena which raise entirely new problems for investigation are discovered during experiments, especially when combinations of conditions are imposed such as never occur in nature or in current technological practice. We cannot foresee such discoveries because we can only imagine things in terms of our past experience and because the response of a plant or animal to conditions never experienced in the course of its evolution is virtually unpredictable—except, that is, when we can confidently predict death. The successful scientist is the one who perceives and takes advantage of his luck and does not throw his experiment away because the result is not the one he was looking for. More really new discoveries are made in so called 'pure' than in 'applied' research because in the latter the treatments too often cover a timidly small range on either side of accepted practice.

Practising scientists do not often consciously work round the cycles shown in Figs. 1–1 and 1–2; the whole process is more intuitive and less tidy. Information and ideas from reading, meetings and conversation are brought in at all stages; half-formulated hypotheses or experimental results that seem to defy interpretation are stored away until some new piece of information illuminates the scene; predictions sometimes cannot be tested until new apparatus, which may even suggest them by its existence, becomes available. Nevertheless I believe that all the stages shown are essential to science.

A summarized account of one of the investigations of Charles and Francis DARWIN (1880) will serve as a model for the methods of experimental science. The Darwins *observed* that the coleoptiles of grass seedlings bent towards light coming from one side, so that the tips pointed straight at the light source; the bend was at first just below the tip but later travelled down the coleoptile, implying a straightening of the upper part. They made the *hypothesis* that the uppermost part of the coleoptile 'determined the direction of curvature of the lower part'; they *predicted* that shielding the tip of the coleoptile from light should prevent bending if their hypothesis was correct but should make no difference if it was false. In modern statistical logic the appropriate so called null hypothesis (p. 12) is that shielding the tips should be without effect. They designed and carried out *experiments* in which seedlings with and without blackened tinfoil caps on their coleoptile tips were unilaterally illuminated. Only the coleoptiles with the uncovered tips bent appreciably towards the light (see Plate 2a in AUDUS, 1959). This *disproved* the null hypothesis and so supported the Darwins' suggestion. From this and the results of many other ingenious experiments they concluded: 'that when seedlings are freely exposed to a lateral light some influence is transmitted from the upper to the lower part, causing the latter to bend'. This 'influence' we now call an auxin or plant hormone.

We may next look in more detail at some aspects of the stages shown in Fig. 1–2.

1.2.1   Observations (natural history)

Casual observation suggests that where plants of wood anemone (*Anemone nemorosa*) have spread from a wood into an adjacent field the leaves tend to be smaller. Measurements on sample plants might establish this difference in average leaf size for the two environments with a degree of confidence depending on its magnitude, consistency and the number of leaves measured; if it appeared well established we should say that environment had influenced the leaf size. This observation would raise a host of problems. though it would not contribute to their solution. For example, is the effect due to the differences between the wood and the field in light intensity, or light quality, or wind speed, or air temperature, or atmospheric humidity, or soil moisture, nitrogen supply or hydrogen ion concentration, or other factors too numerous to mention? More than one of these factors might well contribute to the observed effect. For a single wood there could even be some difference in soil type that happened to follow roughly the boundary but was not connected with the presence or absence of trees, but this hazard could be avoided by measuring leaves within and outside a number of woods. We could also make observations of many of the factors mentioned, by the methods of micrometeorology or soil science, and where they were not consistently different within and outside the wood we should probably assume that they were unimportant in affecting leaf size; for factors showing consistent differences we should be left guessing (making hypotheses) as to their relative importance. Our guessing might be assisted by the finding of a good fit to a straight line relation (high correlation coefficient) between leaf sizes and the intensities of a factor, both measured in a number of different places. This would not, however, show that the factor *caused* the change in leaf size, for both might be linearly related to (correlated with) the true causal factor which we had not measured. For example, light that has passed through leaves is depleted especially in the red and blue spectral regions and has relatively more far red than normal daylight. A linear relation between leaf size and total light intensity, as measured under shade from trees, could be due to a linear relation of both with the proportion of far-red. The connection could be even more remote: light intensity might be linearly related with atmospheric humidity or wind speed, the most shady places being the most sheltered, and one of these might be the main causal factor. There are methods for calculating 'partial correlations' in which the linearity of the relation with one factor can be estimated after eliminating that of the relation with another factor or factors, but we are still left with the possibility of 'spurious correlations'.

Undoubtedly, for most of us, the best way to get ideas for starting an experimental investigation is to do our own natural history. We tend to observe the things that interest us and therefore (generally) are interested in the things we ourselves observe; the problem, when perceived, has then a personal quality and a personal appeal. The field botanist may prefer some problem like the one outlined above. The entomologist may wonder why parasitic hymenoptera congregate on Umbelliferous flowers (van EMDEN, 1963): is it their whiteness, or the shelter of the neighbouring hedgrow, or the height above the ground, or the characteristic scents of the particular mixtures of terpenes? In the garden we may be fascinated by the motile stamens of *Mahonia* or *Berberis*; in the glasshouse by the even more striking movements of *Mimosa pudica* or by the production of plant-lets round the leaf margins of *Bryophyllum calycinum*; in the laboratory by the reproductive gemmae of *Lunularia* or the light sensitivity of *Euglena*. The method is to study the plants or animals that do things that fire our imagination and note the conditions under which they do them; then to make hypotheses as to which are the more important controlling factors in the complex of conditions, with a view to trying them out experimentally, or (more difficult) make hypotheses that can be tested in experiments as to the internal mechanisms.

Another good method, though not so good I think, is to browse in the library. Many books from the turn of the Century (SACHS, 1887; PFEFFER, 1900–3; KERNER, 1902) are full of accounts of intriguing phenomena; so are the more recent books by SKENE (1924) and SALISBURY (1961). These authors were all excellent observers but their natural history should be checked by personal observation before going on to the further stages of hypothesis, prediction and experiment. Conditions may be different, varieties differ in their behaviour, and different observers notice different things.

1.2.2 *Why have a hypothesis?*

As has been implied above, most really new discoveries are made by chance in experiments designed for other purposes. Moreover, I have found that my first hypotheses are more often wrong than correct (e.g. HEATH, 1950) and I believe this is common experience (DARWIN, 1958). Why then should we bother with a hypothesis until after we have dis-covered some new and startling phenomenon by trying this and that and observing what happens? It is a curious fact that such aimless experiments are almost always completely unproductive. The need for a hypothesis, if experiments are to yield new discoveries or even be useful at a less spec-tacular level, is in part psychological. To design and carry out a good experi-ment and to consider the results requires an exacting mental effort, often for long periods. The emotional drive needed to overcome our innate reluctance to think connectedly, and also needed to ensure that the subconscious continues work on the problems when we are otherwise occupied (POINCARÉ, 1914; WALLIS, 1926), is provided by the hope of obtaining evidence to support our own hypothesis or, almost as effective, to disprove someone else's with which we disagree. This hope, and the feeling that the investigation is in some indefinable way important, makes us observe very carefully a certain class of result, so that we do at least see *something*; without a hypothesis to provide the urge and suggest what to observe and record we are likely to see nothing at all.

The hypothesis may indeed prevent us from seeing the significance of other classes of result. For example Darwin crossed the common form of *Antirrhinum* with the peloric (or regular flowered) sort. The F_1 plants were all of the common type and in F_2 there were 88 common to 37 peloric or $2.37:1$, which was a reasonable approximation to $3:1$ for so few plants. Darwin was so imbued with the hypothesis of blending inheritance that he did not realize that it was disproved by these and other similar results in his breeding experiments. The peculiar genius of Mendel was needed to perceive a pattern in the distribution of single pairs of contrasting characters in the F_2 generation, to make a hypothesis of particulate inheritance, and to work out its consequences as a mathematical system (MENDEL, 1965; de BEER, 1964).

Scientific originality is often thought to reside in making new hypotheses: in putting together existing knowledge and ideas in unusual combinations, or so called mavericity. For this to be useful it must be coupled, either in the same person or another, with the ability to plan and execute good experiments to test the hypotheses; here also Mendel excelled.

Often the observations which first suggested a problem, whether made in an experiment or under natural conditions, are found to be inadequate when a hypothesis has been made. It may be necessary to repeat them on a larger scale or with different or more precise measurements to confirm the reality of the supposed phenomenon, or the hypothesis may suggest the need for supplementary information. It is impossible to observe everything and the hypothesis improves our natural history by suggesting what must be observed to increase our understanding of nature.

To say that a hypothesis should be consistent with all the relevant observations (p. 2) is a counsel of perfection. Sometimes it is necessary to use one hypothesis for phenomena of one class and an apparently conflicting hypothesis for those of another. An example is the use of a wave theory of light for many optical phenomena and a 'corpuscular' or particle theory, in which light arrives in discrete packets or 'quanta', for photochemistry. These two theories have been reconciled by wave mechanics, in a mathematical 'wavicle', but they had to be used side by side for years before this synthesis was achieved and are still so used for most purposes.

It may therefore be a mistake to give up a hypothesis too easily in the face of apparently adverse evidence, though to cling to it obstinately can be a dangerous gamble. The 'best' hypothesis is that which, for the time being, fits the greatest variety of observations, that is, provides the widest generalization.

1.2.3 Prediction and design of experiments

These should go together, for it is seldom useful to predict consequences of the hypothesis which would occur under conditions that cannot be provided. As SAWYER (1943) writes: 'Reason is in fact nothing more nor less than an experiment carried out in the imagination', and so we make our predictions by imagining an experiment and the different results it should give if our hypothesis is true or false. It is not enough to imagine the results however, for few of us resemble the dispassionate and completely objective scientist of fiction and we too easily persuade ourselves that the result should be favourable to our hypothesis. The experiment must be carried out. Even so, it is remarkable how often the results seem to the experimenter to support his hypothesis; we all tend to design experiments that will do this and it is therefore worth while to make a conscious effort to avoid bias by including a wide range of conditions which will test the hypothesis severely. This is discussed later.

1.2.4 What is an experiment?

The essence of an experiment is that it enables us to compare the effects of two or more 'treatments' on some attribute of the plants, animals or other experimental material. To provide valid comparisons the material to be given different treatments must be chosen without bias; to be of value the experiment must not only yield information as to the kind and magnitude of the apparent effects of the treatments but also provide an estimate of variability.

As an example let us suppose we wish to test the hypothesis that differences in light intensity, as distinct from light quality, could be responsible for the differences of leaf size in *A. nemorosa* observed within and outside the wood (p. 6). This at once suggests a shading experiment. We might rear a number of plants from 'seed' (achenes) or from rhizomes in pots of soil and then grow some under screens of butter muslin and others in the open. We might record the length of the central lobe of each leaf as giving a measure of leaf size. We should soon find that among the different plants given the same treatment (either shading or no shading) there were appreciable differences in leaf length. Such differences could be due to innumerable factors that we had either not attempted to control or had not equalized completely for all the plants: genetic differences, 'seed' or rhizome size, contact with soil moisture films at germination, depth of sowing, amount of soil in the pot, small differences in temperature, humidity, wind exposure and other meteorological factors in different positions. This list could be extended indefinitely and however careful we were it would be impossible to make conditions exactly the same for all plants. Obviously it would be useless to do an experiment with only one plant in each treatment, for any differences found might be due to *uncontrolled* (*or random*) *variation* of the sort just discussed and in no way connected with the treatments. With a number of plants (*replicates*) for each treatment we could expect that such sources of uncontrolled variation would tend to average out, so that an approximation to the true treatment effects would be shown by the mean values. This could only happen if the plants for each treatment were chosen without bias; if for instance we chose by inspection all the plants for one treatment before we went on to the next, the first treatment would be likely to have most of the best plants and an apparent effect of treatment might be solely due to such an unfair start. To avoid bias we must ensure that every plant to be used in the experiment has an equal chance of having any one of the treatments and this can *only* be done by allotting the treatments to the plants at random i.e. by some such procedure as cutting a well shuffled pack of cards or drawing numbers out of a hat, or from special tables of random numbers so prepared. If the treatments have been allotted in this way, the amount of variation observed among similarly treated plants ('within treatments') will give a valid estimate of the uncontrolled variation that may be expected to affect the comparison between means for differently treated plants ('between treatments'). We can then calculate the chances of the differences we observe between treatments being solely due to uncontrolled variation. We will consider how this is done (*tests of significance*) in the next chapter.

Our shading experiment would virtually eliminate the possibility that any effect of the light treatments was acting through light quality; as an extra precaution we could use nylon or perforated zinc screens instead of muslin, as moulds growing on the latter might change the colour of the light and would certainly alter the degree of shading. However, there would remain other '*confounded effects*' of the treatment. For example, the screens would inevitably reduce air movements and therefore water loss from the plants and soil; indeed the reduction in light intensity would itself have the latter effects. Difference in soil moisture is one of the factors considered as possibly causing different leaf sizes within and outside the wood (p. 6) and we might decide to include this in the experiment. Half the pots with shading and half those without could be watered frequently so that the soil was at all times moist, while the others could be watered only when the plants began to wilt. (Better methods of deciding when to water can be based on loss in weight but the problem is not a simple one: HUDSON, 1957). We should then have four *combination treatments* in what is called a *factorial experiment*. We could of course have several degrees of shading combined with several frequencies of watering but for simplicity we will discuss only two of each. The data could be tabulated as below.

The desired treatments are stated first and those actually applied are shown in brackets. This will be discussed in the next section.

Such a set of four treatment means (*a*, *b*, *c* and *d*) contains four independent items of information. They can be rearranged mathematically in

| | Mean leaf lengths from N plants | | |
	Low light (shaded)	High light (not shaded)	Mean
Low soil moisture (watered seldom)	a	b	$\dfrac{a+b}{2}$
High soil moisture (watered often)	c	d	$\dfrac{c+d}{2}$
Mean	$\dfrac{a+c}{2}$	$\dfrac{b+d}{2}$	$\dfrac{a+b+c+d}{4}$

various ways, with the object of making their meaning more easily under-stood, to yield four, but no more than four, independent quantities. If we rearrange the data to give fewer than four independent quantities we are not making use of all the information contained in the experiment; if more than four, the quantities cannot all be independent and we are likely to deceive ourselves into thinking we have more information than there is. We have in fact four, and only four, *degrees of freedom*. The most generally useful way of re-grouping the treatment means from such a 2 × 2 factorial experiment is as follows:

$$(a+b+c+d)/4 = W \qquad (1.1)$$
$$\{(b+d)-(a+c)\}/2 = X \qquad (1.2)$$
$$\{(c+d)-(a+b)\}/2 = Y \qquad (1.3)$$
$$\{(d-c)-(b-a)\}/2 = \{(d-b)-(c-a)\}/2$$
$$= \{(d+a)-(b+c)\}/2 = Z \qquad (1.4)$$

The difference between two numbers is independent of their sum; for example, two numbers having a difference of 5 could have a sum anywhere between $+\infty$ and $-\infty$. The first equation may be looked upon as the sum of $(a+c)$ and $(b+d)$, while the second is their difference. Therefore X is independent of W and by a similar argument X, Y and Z are all independent of W and of each other.

W is the *general mean* of all the observations and the first of our four degrees of freedom has thus been used in calculating the general mean. The other degrees of freedom may be said to represent *independent com-parisons* among the data. With N items there are possible $N-1$ comparisons independent of the mean and of each other; for this reason there are usually said to be $N-1$ degrees of freedom, but this excludes the one used for the mean. We will return to W when we have considered X, Y and Z.

X is the difference between the mean for all the 'high light' leaves and that for all the 'low light' ones. It is therefore the *mean effect of light intensity* averaged over both soil moisture treatments; this effect will be positive if high light has increased leaf length and negative if it has reduced

it. We have supposed that this experiment was started to test the hypothesis that shading increased leaf length (a negative effect of light intensity)
but when faced with results it is apparent that this hypothesis was not
precise. We are in no position to say *how much* the amount of shading we
have given should increase leaf length and even if we had some idea we
could never state a length exactly. Therefore, although we expect (and
probably hope) that shading will have increased leaf length we make the
converse and only precise hypothesis available, namely that shading is
without effect on length, so that the 'true' (hypothetical) increase should
be zero. This is called a *null hypothesis* but, as that name is used for *any*
precise hypothesis tested in an experiment, we will distinguish it as a *zero
hypothesis*; such a hypothesis has generally to be made for experiments
where the data can vary continuously, as can weights, lengths and areas.
The comparison with hypothesis appropriate to the degree of freedom for
X is:

$$\frac{(b+d)-(a+c)}{2}-\text{o} = X \qquad\qquad (cf. \textbf{1.2} \text{ p. } 11)$$

If X is less than zero a negative effect of light intensity is indicated. We
must then compare the magnitude of this negative value with an estimate
of the amount of uncontrolled or random variation in order to calculate the
chances of random variation alone giving a negative *or* positive effect as
large as, or larger than, that observed. If this is found to be very improbable
the zero hypothesis is considered to be disproved, at the calculated level
of probability; an effect of light is therefore supported.

Y is the *mean effect of soil moisture* averaged over both light treatments.
It may be expected to be positive, that is leaf length is likely to be greater
at the high soil moisture.

Z is rather less straightforward. $(d-c)$ is the effect of (or response to)
light intensity with high soil moisture and $(b-a)$ is the response to light
intensity with low soil moisture. The first form in which Z is shown in the
equation is therefore half the difference in the responses to light at high and
low soil moisture; as shown, this is equal to the second form of the equation
which gives Z as half the difference in the responses to soil moisture at high
and low light. Both these forms are equal to the third, which is calculated
as the difference of the means of the diagonals in the two-way table. The
value of Z is the *interaction effect* for light and soil moisture; it will be
positive if increasing one factor produces a greater positive, or smaller
negative, response at high level of the other factor than at low, and negative
if it produces a smaller positive or larger negative response. Again we make
the hypothesis that the interaction effect should be zero. If this is not disproved, the results are consistent with absence of interaction, that is with
the effects of the two factors being quite independent and therefore additive. If Z is zero, $(d-c)=(b-a)$ so that the response to light is the same at
either soil moisture level, and similarly the response to soil moisture is the

same at either light intensity; the combined effect of both factors at high level is equal to the sum of their separate effects i.e. $(d-a)=(b-a)+(c-a)$. Such lack of interaction is uncommon but when it occurs it suggests that the two factors act on quite different systems in the plant. If the interaction effect is not zero, its sign and magnitude are often of great interest. We might find a much larger negative response to light intensity at high soil moisture than at low and a negative interaction would then be shown:

$(d-c) < (b-a)$, and therefore Z, or $\dfrac{(d-c)-(b-a)}{2}$, would be negative.

For example, if $a=4$, $b=2$, $c=11$ and $d=5$, Z is -4. We might then suppose that at low soil moisture the full effect of low light was unable to show because of lack of water for cell expansion.

For discovering such often important interactions factorial experiments provide a powerful and indeed the only available tool; at the same time the mean effect of each factor is estimated as accurately as if an experiment of the same size had been devoted to it alone.

We may now return to W. The zero hypothesis states that the mean leaf length should be zero, which is patently absurd, but we have no more reasonable precise hypothesis to put in its place. The appropriate comparison with this hypothesis is:

$$\frac{a+b+c+d}{4} - o = W \qquad\qquad (cf.\ \text{1.1 p. 11})$$

For many statistical processes it is desirable to have the general mean representing one of the degrees of freedom and this limits the choice of possible sets of independent comparisons.

Serial experiments. In the experiment just discussed it has been supposed that the different treatments were applied to the plants at the same time. This would have the advantage that, apart from effects due to the treatments themselves, all the plants would have the same sort of weather. On the other hand the treatments had to be spread out in space and applied to different plants, with the possibilities already mentioned of genetic variation, differences in time of germination, in early growth, and so forth. If the differences between the treatment responses of individual plants or animals are expected to be large it may be thought better for the treatments to be applied in succession to the same individual, i.e. to be spread out in time instead of in space; the uncontrolled variation due to individuality incorporated in the treatment comparisons will then be reduced, but that due to such factors as weather and age will be increased; there is also the serious hazard of after-effects of earlier treatments upon the responses to subsequent ones. Such serial experiments are often used in investigations with large and expensive animals such as dairy cows; for example, to test the effects of different diets upon milk yield. Whichever method is used for the treatments, the replicates may be arranged in space or in time or both.

Experiments on pairs. A better method of reducing the uncontrolled variation in the treatment comparisons is the '*paired sample method*'. With only
two treatments, pairs of plants (or animals) are selected which match as
closely as conveniently obtainable in respect of some attribute or attributes
considered important. (A particularly favourable case is the use of identical
twin calves.) The two treatments are then allotted to the members of each
pair at random. The different pairs can vary widely and if they do the mean
of the treatment effects found within the pairs will be of wider application;
if they cover too wide a range, however, the results from the different pairs
may be so variable that the null hypothesis is not disproved and no treatment effect can be demonstrated. This method can be extended to more
than two treatments and will be discussed further in Chapter 3.

Genetical and other trials. There is another quite different type of experiment that is used extensively in genetics, in which the comparison is made
not between the results of two or more treatments but between the observed
result of a single kind of event and a predicted result based on theory. It
thus resembles what I have called observational science but the event or
set of circumstances that is to test the hypothesis is now brought about
by the experimenter instead of being provided by nature. This type of
experiment I shall distinguish as a *trial*. A good example is provided by the
earliest trials made by Mendel. In 1856 (de BEER, 1964) Mendel started
systematic crosses between the pea varieties that he had been testing for the
previous two years. Crossing a round seeded variety with one that had
wrinkled seeds when ripe yielded nothing but round seeds; 253 hybrid
plants grown from these in 1857 and selfed produced 7324 seeds, 5474 of
which were round and 1850 wrinkled, giving a ration of 2·96 to 1. Similarly,
the cross yellow cotyledons × green cotyledons made in 1856 produced only
yellow seeds which in 1857 gave a ratio of 3·01 yellow to 1 green. This
presumably unexpected observation, or perhaps an earlier somewhat
similar one not published, corresponds to stage 1 of Figs. 1–1 and 1–2.
Mendel explained it by assuming that particles controlling heredity
[genes], which were present in pairs [alleles] in both parents, segregated in
the germ cells; that all germ cells were equally likely to achieve fertilization
and that both sexes made an equal contribution to the offspring. Hence,
in the symbols now used:

$$AA \times aa$$
$$\downarrow$$
$$Aa + Aa \qquad \qquad F_1$$
$$Aa \times Aa \rightarrow AA + 2Aa + aa \qquad F_2$$

With A completely dominant over a, this gave a ratio of 3:1. This prediction was supported in further trials, but in 1858 Mendel also showed that
the 3:1 ratio was made up of 1:2:1. 565 round seeds obtained in F_2 as
shown above produced 193 plants that bred true when selfed, giving
nothing but round seeds, and 372 that segregated again into round and

wrinkled—a ratio of $1:1.93$ (See de BEER, 1964, for further discussion of these results).

Null hypotheses. In such trials the null hypothesis is not a zero hypothesis but it can be stated precisely because it is in the form of a mathematical relation which specifies the *association* between two (or more) variables: in the example just considered a *ratio* of the number of round to the number of wrinkled peas. Similarly we can make an exact hypothesis for the proportions in which oxygen and hydrogen atoms will combine under a specified set of conditions. These examples are for discontinuous variates, which can only vary by discrete steps (whole numbers in the above cases) but we can also set up precise hypotheses for the association between two or more continuous variates like weight, length, area, time. We may make the hypothesis that the weight of a growing plant or animal should be related to time by a linear, exponential or other type of mathematical equation; or that the growth of a part and the whole should have a particular type of mathematical relation (HEATH, 1937). Any such hypothesis can be directly tested in a trial with only one treatment. On the other hand in most experiments on the effect of different treatments on a single variate the only precise hypothesis is that the treatments have been entirely without effect, though there can be very few treatments for which we would believe this; if the experiment disproves the zero hypothesis it supports the alternative, and imprecise, hypothesis that the treatments have had an effect. Exceptions occur when the treatments are themselves considered as variates: a hypothesis stating the type of mathematical relation between yield and amount of nitrogenous fertilizer could be directly tested in an experiment with nitrogen supplied at several different rates, or in a factorial experiment we could directly test the hypothesis that the interaction effect was not zero but had some specified mathematical form.

1.2.5 Interpretation

What is a treatment, or whodunnit? A treatment as applied in an experiment is never simple, in the sense that it alters only one factor, although this is usually what the experimenter intends. In our hypothetical shading experiment the intention was that the two shading treatments (with and without screens) should differ only in light intensity. We have already noted that an effect of the screens on air movement would tend to restrict water loss but this is only one of an indefinitely large number of confounded treatment effects. Humidity of the air, temperatures of the air, plants and soil are four factors that would differ under the screens and in the open. If the experiment was out of doors, the screens would reduce the amount of rain falling on the shaded plants and probably cause drips which would puddle the soil. Obviously, however carefully we tried to equalize the watering in each watering treatment, the resulting soil moisture contents would only be the same (nearly) in the shaded and unshaded pots immediately after watering. Our watering treatments would not in fact be independent of our shading treatments and this would probably of itself result in the data showing an interaction. The watering treatments would have further confounded effects of their own. If we used hard tap water we should add more calcium and magnesium salts to the frequently watered pots; if we avoided this by using rainwater we should still leach more nutrients out of them; even if we collected and returned the drainage effluent there would still result differences in the physical packing and aeration of the soil due to the frequency of watering.

It may be objected that such complexities do not arise in the less 'earthy' and more fundamental branches of biology; if so, consider the apparently simple problem of supplying tissue cultures with different amounts of potassium ion. Unfortunately, potassium ions cannot be obtained except with the equivalent anions. Potassium hydroxide can be used, to avoid adding chlorine or some other such anion, but this will affect the pH. Probably the medium will incorporate a buffer, but then the added OH^- ions will alter the proportions of certain ions and undissociated molecules in the buffer mixture. Again, if we vary the amount of potassium we alter the total concentration of solutes, unless we simultaneously vary some other solute (perhaps a sodium salt) which may then be responsible for the observed effects. Further, we change the ratios of potassium to all the other ions present and the ratios (or 'balance') of two or more kinds of ions may be the most important factor.

I believe that the limit to the number of such confounded effects for *any* experimental treatment is set only by our knowledge and powers of imagination. An experiment in which the application of treatments to the material under investigation has been properly randomized can yield an unbiased estimate of the effects of those treatments *as applied*; it gives no information as to which of the myriad components in any treatment comparison are responsible for the effects observed. That is a question of interpretation and is entirely a matter for the experimenter's judgement.

At this stage the reader may think that the experimentalist is no better off than the observational scientist guessing at the important components of the complex of natural conditions and looking for correlations. There is, however, this difference. For the observational scientist the 'treatments' which test his predictions are provided by nature and he can seldom eliminate a confounded component which he may consider important; the experimental scientist can design his experiments so as to eliminate or reduce *some*, though at the cost of introducing or increasing others. Our perforated zinc shades would have practically no effect on light quality but as we have seen would have a number of other 'side effects'.

The method is to think of as many as possible of the confounded components of the desired treatments and decide first which are unlikely to be important and may be neglected. Of those that seem important we try to eliminate the ones that are not too difficult and then do some experiments. In subsequent experiments we may arrange for *different* changes of conditions to be confounded with the desired treatments and so test our judgement of their importance.

For example, I wished to test the hypothesis that long days had a specific effect (not acting through the amount of photosynthesis) in causing onion plants to bulb. The method of observational science would have been first, to observe that onion plants in England normally make bulbs in late spring as the days lengthen. However, at the same time light intensities and temperatures increase; these and the lengthening days must all result in more photosynthesis. Different combinations of light intensities and daylengths could have been obtained by observation at different latitudes but these would be confounded with large temperature differences. In particular, the tropics would have provided short days with high light intensity. European varieties of onion have been found not to bulb in the tropics and sub-tropics which suggests that amount of photosynthesis is not so important as daylength, but of course large differences in temperature and many other factors are involved in the comparison with England.

The simplest form of experiment would have been in summer to place dark covers over half the onion plants each night from say 4 p.m. to 7 a.m. making a day of 9 hours (Short Day Treatment), and leave the other half exposed to the natural long days, of about 16 hours (Long Day Treatment). The Long Day plants would then have had 7 extra hours of photosynthesis and, if they bulbed more than the Short Day plants, this could have been a 'nutritional' effect.

This difference in photosynthesis could have been reduced by placing muslin screens over the Long Day plants when the Short Day plants were darkened. Even so the plants under the dark covers would have been at higher temperatures and atmospheric humidities. For my experiment, therefore, I decided to give the plants of both treatments 9 hours of daylight each day and then transfer them to similar light-tight ventilated chambers; here the Long Day plants received 7 hours and the Short Day plants $3\frac{1}{2}$ hours of further illumination with low intensity incandescent electric light, at such a value that photosynthesis would scarcely exceed respiration, if at all. Note that a difference in photosynthetic effect must still have existed during the extra $3\frac{1}{2}$ hours light, for in the Long Day plants some of the respiratory losses in this period would have been made good by photosynthesis, in the Short Day plants none. I hoped that this difference was negligible, but another important effect would have been confounded with the Long Day treatment: the electric light raised the temperature considerably in the chambers, and temperature was known to have large effects on bulbing. Anticipating this, I fitted compensating electric heaters, working at black heat, in the Short Day chambers. These came on when the Short Day lamps went off and went off when the Long Day lamps did so. This kept air temperatures nearly the same in the two treatments. I then judged other confounded effects to be sufficiently irrelevant to justify some experiments. In view of the importance of temperature I included two

glasshouse temperature treatments also in a factorial design (details in
HEATH, 1943b).

My compensating heaters brought in a new confounded effect. The Long
Day plants received an extra $3\frac{1}{2}$ hours daily of visible radiation and to this
I attributed the fact that they made bulbs, but during this period the Short
Day plants were receiving more infra-red radiation and this might have
been inhibiting bulbing. This possibility could of course have been investigated in further experiments. Some twenty-five years later one of my
students found that the wave length of radiation used to extend the daylength was indeed important for the bulbing of onions, though we did not
investigate effects of infra-red.

We see that the common criticism of other people's experiments ('this
was not a truly controlled comparison'), that the units receiving different
desired treatments had also different something else, must always be true
except of experiments whose aim was completely empirical.

What is a control?   There seems to be a good deal of mystique about controls,
but a control is in fact simply an individual or batch of material given one
of the treatments in an experiment; this *control treatment* is usually chosen
as being in some way the normal or 'natural' treatment, which may of
course be a zero treatment. This is an excellent practice in so far as it
results in the range of any factor, varied in a series of treatments, including
a level to which the organism is adapted. It has been mentioned earlier
that subjecting organisms to conditions that they have never experienced
in evolution can result in quite unexpected phenomena but this is only
useful if we can compare them with the usual state of affairs. Often, extensive series of investigations are carried out entirely at 'unphysiological'
levels of such factors as oxygen or carbon dioxide concentration, because
of the demands of convenient or very sensitive techniques, and then the
results obtained can be quite misleading (HEATH, 1969, p. 265).

A less admirable aspect of the inclusion of a control treatment in an
experiment is that there is often a tendency to compare the results of each
of the other treatments individually with the control. This procedure can
introduce a bias into the results because the comparisons are not independent: if the mean for the controls is determined with only the same
precision as each of the other treatment means, and it happens by chance
to be, for example, particularly large, each of the other treatments will tend
to show a very small positive or large negative effect. Such comparisons
can vitiate the tests of significance usually applied.

Levels of interpretation.   So far I have only mentioned the interpretation of
the applied treatment—*which* are the most effective components out of all
the confounded changes made? Our choices among these should depend on
our hypotheses on the more fundamental question of *how* these changes of
conditions bring about the observed effect. Often we are in no position to
make rational hypotheses and must rely on empirical knowledge or even

guess-work but the ultimate aim must be to interpret observed effects in terms of the internal mechanisms of the plant or animal. This can be done at various levels of organization and depends usually on the level investigated in the experiment. The phenomena observed in any experiment are generally interpreted at what might be termed the next level in order of reducing complexity. The results of a shading experiment applied to a mixed natural community of plants would probably be 'explained' on the basis of known growth responses to light intensity of the individual species when growing in isolation or even in pure stands. This would involve a great many simplifying assumptions about the degree of shading of one species by another, and hence such things as relative heights, geometry of leaf arrangement, and so forth. In general, the bigger the change of level from the experiment to the interpretation the more simplifying assumptions are needed and if the step is too large these become absurd, as for instance if an explanation of the growth responses in the above experiment were attempted in terms of electron transfer in photosynthesis. However, such an attempt might be quite appropriate for an experiment on light intensity and photosynthesis in isolated chloroplasts. The results of the shading experiment with potted plants of *A. nemorosa* discussed earlier might well be interpreted in terms of cell division and cell extension.

As the system studied is progressively simplified, ecology becomes animal or plant physiology and these in turn become biochemistry and physical chemistry. The gain in apparent simplicity is accompanied by increasing doubt as to whether the findings apply to what happens in the community or intact organism. Experiments should therefore be carried out at all levels, chosen according to the interests and abilities of the investigator. Results obtained in the simpler systems may 'explain' those in the more complex; the latter may show whether or not the simpler system is relevant and, moreover, provide a continual supply of new phenomena to be explained.

Dating experiments. All biological material varies in time and it is important that all experiments should be dated. The dates should be looked upon as an essential part of the description of the treatments and any publication should include them. The reasons for this have been elaborated elsewhere (HEATH, 1967); the date of an experiment is probably more useful than any other single item of information in helping later workers to interpret experimental results in the light of further knowledge. For example, the germination of groundsel seeds, imbibed with water, is promoted by light given soon after they are shed but this sensitivity to light disappears in time. With this knowledge it is of interest to examine published data on the light sensitivity of other seeds and look for differences between results obtained in autumn and in spring. Such comparisons are impossible with undated experiments; they become much more precise if harvest dates are also given.

1.2.6   Practical difficulties

In almost all experimental investigations quite unforeseen difficulties occur. It is therefore important at an early stage to carry out preliminary tests to see if the plants or animals will do what is required of them under the conditions proposed for the experiment. It might be found that *A. nemorosa* 'seed' germinated so irregularly that it was impossible with facilities available to obtain enough plants of even roughly similar size. This would necessitate either finding another method of propagation (e.g. rhizomes), trying another plant (often the best plan) or investigating the conditions needed for germination. This last investigation could well develop into the main project. Cultivated plants have usually been selected for even germination; many wild species, however, have evolved patterns of germination spread out over long periods, thus improving the chances that *some* seedlings will survive, or occurring only in response to special stimuli such as exposure to light or a period of low temperature when in an imbibed condition.

Details of technique satisfactory with one species may be disastrous with another. Some plants are severely damaged by water dripping off galvanized wire netting and would therefore also presumably suffer under perforated zinc. Again, although some plants, such as radish or wheat, will grow perfectly well in water culture without any aeration of the solution, others such as onion need continuous aeration.

1.2.7   Disproof of, or support for, the hypothesis

A zero hypothesis can obviously never be proved, for subsequent experiments with more replicates or more accurate measurements may show effects of the treatments and so disprove it. Similarly a hypothesis for the mathematical relation between two variates can never be proved to be correct in any trial, but only supported or disproved. However, they can only be disproved in the sense that it is shown to be extremely improbable that they are true. We calculate the chances of an apparent treatment effect, or a deviation from the proposed relation, as large as or larger than that found, being solely due to uncontrolled variation. If the odds are very small, say 1 in 20, we may consider this so unlikely that we reject the zero hypothesis and conclude that the effects observed are at least partly due to the treatments, or that the true relation is really different from that postulated; we say that the effects, or deviation, are 'significant'. However, on the average, once in every 20 experiments or trials that yield these odds we shall be wrong; even if we decide only to accept odds of 1 in 10^6 we shall not achieve certainty. As R. A. FISHER wrote in *The Design of Experiments*: '... no isolated experiment, however significant in itself, can suffice for the experimental demonstration of any natural phenomenon; for the 'one chance in a million' will undoubtedly occur, with no less and no more than its appropriate frequency, however surprised we may be that it should occur to *us*. In order to assert that a natural phenomenon is experimentally demonstrable we need, not an isolated record, but a reliable method of procedure. In relation to the test of significance, we may say that a phenomenon is experimentally demonstrable when we know how to conduct an experiment that will rarely fail to give us a statistically significant result' (loc. cit. p.13).

The particular value of repeating experiments in time will be discussed further in Chapter 3.

There is a curious antithesis, already implied, between a zero hypothesis and all other precise hypotheses: if the experimental results fail to disprove, and so support, the zero hypothesis we usually feel that the experiment has failed in its object and are disappointed, but if a trial fails to disprove and so supports the correctness of a postulated relation between two variates we consider that it has succeeded. This is doubtless because we usually disbelieve the zero hypothesis and would like to believe in the mathematical relation; the converse situation can apply if we are testing some other worker's hypotheses!

Magnitude of effects. An effect of treatment, or a deviation from a postulated mathematical relation, may be shown to be so unlikely to be due to random variation as to be almost certainly real ('highly significant'); they may nevertheless be so small as to be of no practical importance and only of theoretical interest if we can produce convincing hypotheses to account for them. It is important, therefore, to estimate their magnitude and, since such estimates are subject to random variation, to calculate the limits within which they would probably be found in other similar experiments ('confidence limits'). It is not uncommon for experimenters to be so delighted at finding 'significant' effects that they fail to consider their size or importance.

1.2.8   What to do with the literature

It is most desirable, especially at the beginning of an investigation, to have personal access to a good library. Reading by post is slow and frustrating. The value of browsing as a method of finding intriguing subjects for investigation has already been mentioned and it may also, of course, illuminate later stages. Once a subject has been chosen we need to find out something of what has already been done by other workers. Here there is a difficult balance to achieve between reading too little and reading too much. In order to advance scientific knowledge we should not, in general, start our investigations too far back from the frontiers. On the other hand the attempt to read everything relevant to a proposed investigation defeats its own end, both because in most subjects the number of publications is impossibly large and because it produces an inhibiting conviction that everything has already been done. The danger of modern methods of information retrieval is less that something will be missed than that so much will be retrieved that the recipient will feel like the sorcerer's apprentice.

In this situation there is an increasing temptation to use reviews, most of which are uncritical, and even worse to use abstracts, not for their proper purpose which is to direct the reader to the original papers but as sources of scientific information. Since they inevitably give most prominence to conclusions, give little information about methods and omit nearly all the 'ifs and buts', the impression is heightened that nothing remains to be done.

It is important to discover at the outset who has made large contributions in the proposed field. If this cannot be achieved by gossip (now the principal means of communication between scientists, according to an article in the *New Scientist*), it must be found from the abstracting journals or from reviews. On the plant side, *Horticultural Abstracts* has a wide coverage and is less daunting than *Biological Abstracts*. Review volumes such as the *Annual Review of Plant Physiology* should also be looked at. It may be necessary to go back 20 or 25 years; even if only two or three important words are looked up in the abstract indexes (for instance '*Anemone nemorosa*', 'light intensity' and 'shade') this is a large task. After at least two separate workers or groups have been found in this way I think it better to go to their original papers and get further references from these.

In some such way we might come across the work of G. E. Blackman and his co-workers, who have made extensive use of shading treatments. Their papers would suggest many details of technique, for instance the use of perforated zinc screens (which were, however, greased to avoid zinc toxicity), and would also introduce us to the subject of growth analysis, which could be followed further in the references given if it was new to us. The comprehensive investigation of the ecology of the bluebell by BLACKMAN and RUTTER (1946–50) would give us among other things the surprising information that shading, although it increases the area of bluebell leaves, does not affect their dry weight appreciably (BLACKMAN and RUTTER, 1948). This would at once suggest that we ought to devise some way of estimating the areas of the *Anemone* leaves and should also determine their dry weights.

The rather haphazard methods of using the literature that I have suggested will undoubtedly result in important papers being missed. However, it is much better to carry out an experiment in ignorance that it has already been done by someone else than to spend so long searching the literature that one does no experiments at all. Indeed, repetition is scientifically most valuable. Different workers very seldom design and carry out an experiment in exactly the same way; different confounded components in the treatments are therefore almost inevitable. If in spite of this the results are the same, they are shown to be of wider application. It is disappointing to find that one is not after all a pioneer, but such completely independent confirmation of results is so much more valuable than confirmation by the same worker that a feeling of virtue should be some compensation. If the results are not confirmatory this is a great stimulus to further work by both parties.

Variation

For the results of an experiment, or even of a single observation, to be of scientific value they must be repeatable but it is generally found that however many precautions are taken to repeat the experiment or observation in the same way, the numerical results of the repetitions show a certain amount of variation. This only fails to show if the scale of measurement used is so coarse as to conceal all variation; for example, no variation would be found in the heights of men measured to the nearest fathom. Such variation is attributed to a multitude of factors which the experimenter did not control; since these factors act in either direction and with various effectiveness they are considered to act at random and the variation they produce is the *random or uncontrolled variation* already mentioned. This is a fundamental characteristic of all observations and the basis of all statistical methods. It is essential to be able to estimate the magnitude of the random variation affecting the results of an experiment, in order to decide whether it is likely to account for the apparent effects of the treatments (pp. 9–10).

2.1 Random variation in material

Table 1 shows the fresh weights of 399 radish plants grown at 1 in. × 1 in. (2·5 × 2·5 cm) spacing in four square plastic basins of well mixed compost and treated as uniformly as was practicable. This is called a *uniformity trial* and dummy treatments can be allotted to the data in various ways to try out different experimental designs. The weights vary from less than 0·05 g (shown as 0·0) to over 23 g. Most of the very large plants were round the edges and this suggests that one important source of variation might have been competition for light. For experimental purposes it would probably be better, therefore, to grow the plants in separate pots, well spaced out, unless we deliberately intended to include competition effects, when we should probably omit the edge plants from the experiment and work only with inner plants which were all subjected to similar competition. Suppose we had wished to compare the effects on growth in total fresh weight, under the latter conditions, of placing on the leaves micro-drops of 50 per cent alcohol or of an alcoholic solution of the growth substance gibberellic acid. We might have decided to use the 16 inner plants in the two rows running east and west across the centre of basin II and applied the treatments 3 weeks before the data were collected. If 8 plants were to receive gibberellic acid (GA) and 8 plain 50 per cent alcohol (symbol (1) denoting basal treatment) it would be appropriate to decide which treatment each plant in turn was to have by tossing a coin or looking up odd and even numbers in

Table 1   Fresh weight (g) of radish plants, seed wetted 15.2.68, pricked out 2·5 × 2·5 cm in 4 plastic basins (I–IV) of compost 17.2.68, and harvested 25–6.3.68. (Data of Heath and ter Veer—unpublished)

I   25.3.68

9·7	2·5	8·6	4·5	2·4	14·6	6·4	11·4	6·7	15·9
10·3	10·0	8·8	2·8	1·2	10·0	9·8	1·7	3·2	18·6
4·9	3·8	5·2	10·6	10·6	2·8	3·4	9·5	7·1	7·7
4·5	1·5	2·1	6·2	6·4	3·6	11·1	14·1	3·9	2·7
18·9	6·4	3·2	4·2	13·6	0·9	2·9	2·3	9·4	7·7
8·9	3·2	1·9	1·9	3·0	2·5	1·2	4·8	9·2	1·6
9·6	10·3	2·9	5·0	6·7	6·2	3·3	7·3	5·2	2·1
3·0	9·3	11·6	1·1	3·2	6·8	0·8	12·4	11·4	3·9
11·1	9·3	3·3	7·8	4·2	6·1	2·7	16·2	6·6	12·1
10·7	2·9	3·6	5·2	11·2	10·7	12·0	17·4	2·2	15·6

II   26.3.68

11·9	9·5	4·0	13·6	6·0	6·0	6·5	6·7	12·4	5·6
18·3	4·3	12·1	9·7	3·4	4·1	10·4	0·5	5·2	23·1
15·2	2·9	1·9	5·6	4·2	1·2	9·3	4·5	5·0	15·3
8·9	2·4	3·2	2·3	1·7	2·9	0·1	1·8	8·3	8·5
2·4	12·7	2·5	2·9	8·3	4·4	4·0	12·8	7·1	10·3
10·1	7·9	2·2	8·3	2·3	9·6	7·9	6·9	3·2	11·4
2·0	13·0	3·1	2·2	3·1	5·5	2·4	1·5	10·5	12·9
12·5	2·3	3·8	10·5	2·5	8·6	1·4	11·9	13·2	19·5
3·1	10·2	3·2	8·9	4·7	10·7	13·2	6·2	7·4	13·6
16·4	5·0	8·3	11·5	14·3	0·3	10·6	7·5	5·7	9·3

III   26.3.68

13·9	2·1	8·1	12·4	2·2	5·7	0·4	15·6	3·9	11·5
4·9	9·0	15·4	11·0	1·9	7·2	8·0	7·1	6·0	1·9
8·4	1·9	4·5	16·1	5·5	0·5	11·7	0·5	8·8	13·9
11·3	2·8	11·4	0·8	8·4	9·4	6·5	0·0	7·5	14·0
6·7	9·1	1·3	0·9	10·1	4·6	2·9	3·4	11·0	10·3
0·4	6·8	4·9	2·2	5·4	2·3	5·1	1·4	5·3	3·9
19·9	1·4	1·0	5·6	2·5	3·1	12·4	9·1	11·1	1·5
6·8	0·9	1·5	2·3	—	2·7	5·0	0·1	2·3	11·4
8·3	18·9	2·1	4·1	7·4	2·0	4·7	5·1	3·2	2·9
13·8	4·7	10·1	9·8	18·0	14·4	9·7	8·1	13·6	22·3

IV 26.3.68

20·0	16·7	1·2	5·5	0·8	8·1	8·4	9·4	5·4	15·0
7·2	13·0	0·5	10·5	6·2	11·3	0·7	2·2	16·7	13·3
4·8	13·0	1·2	7·4	8·0	9·2	11·7	2·9	14·8	8·7
15·2	1·8	3·1	3·2	7·0	18·4	1·9	7·8	4·8	11·3
15·6	1·6	2·1	10·2	0·4	12·2	2·0	2·8	10·3	12·7
7·8	5·6	6·0	1·4	1·2	3·5	1·4	2·3	0·7	14·9
14·1	2·3	3·9	5·3	4·7	4·0	11·0	3·0	4·6	13·1
1·3	2·1	7·9	6·7	1·8	4·1	2·0	3·7	10·3	9·6
12·8	10·6	4·9	11·5	3·7	9·0	4·1	5·7	14·0	15·9
14·5	12·2	7·3	6·9	12·3	10·5	6·5	8·0	7·4	6·3

a table of random numbers (FISHER and YATES, 1963, or LINDLEY and MILLER, 1964). Obviously, as soon as one of the treatments had been allotted to 8 plants the remaining plants would have to have the other. Carrying out this exercise on the data yielded the following as the fresh weights for the two fictitious 'treatments':

'Treatment'	(GA)	(1)
	12·7	2·9
	2·5	4·4
	8·3	4·0
	12·8	7·1
	7·9	2·2
	8·3	2·3
	6·9	9·6
	3·2	7·9
Sum	62·6	40·4
Mean	7·83	5·05

If we had obtained this result in an actual experiment, at first sight we might attribute the more than 50 per cent difference in mean fresh weight to the effect of GA. However, we see that such a difference can occur in actual data owing to random variation alone, in the absence of any possible treatment effect. With practice we learn to note the magnitude of the range within each treatment and the degree of overlap of the values in one treatment with those in the other; these are so large in the above example that it would be unnecessary to go through the calculations of a statistical test of significance. When these calculations are made they in fact show that a difference between means as large as, or larger than, that found would be expected to occur due to random variation alone, in such samples from a single population (see below), once in every five to ten experiments. This is probable enough to make it very unsafe to attribute the difference to the effect of the 'treatments'.

2.2   Samples and populations

If we had taken a different pair of rows for the dummy experiment just discussed we should probably have obtained a somewhat different result; indeed this would also be true of the plants in the same two rows differently randomized—if the first plants in the two 'treatments' had happened to be interchanged, with the others as before, the 'treatment' means would have been GA 6·60 and (1) 6·53, a difference of 1 per cent. It seems obvious that the larger the number of plants involved the smaller such chance irregularities in the means are likely to be, as large and small plants will tend to average out; if we allotted 128 of the 255 inner plants in the 4 basins to GA and the other 127 to (1) we might expect the difference between the means due to random variation to be smaller, though it would be unlikely to be *exactly* zero. (One such randomized trial gave GA, 5·50; (1), 6·18; a difference of 12 per cent.) Obviously the 'true' difference between the mean results of the fictitious treatments should be zero but we could only rely on obtaining this true value, undisturbed by random variation, if we weighed an indefinitely large number of plants.

Since successive sets of 8 plants yield different mean values owing to random variation, they are to be considered as *samples* of the available 255 inner plants, and these in turn should be regarded as a sample from an indefinitely large (or 'unlimited') possible *population* of similar plants. Our real interest is seldom in the mean weight of a sample that we happen to have taken but in the 'true' mean weight for the whole population. Similarly, in an experiment with two treatments, such as GA and (1), we want to know whether the plants in both really belong to the same population as in a uniformity trial, so that the true mean is the same for both and we make this our zero hypothesis (p. 12). Disproof at a given level of significance (p. 20) of the zero hypothesis involves showing that the plants in the two treatments are unlikely (at stated odds) to represent samples from the same population—this implies a real effect of treatment.

It is obviously impossible to weigh or measure all the individual plants, animals or other objects comprising an unlimited or indefinitely large population; however, statistical methods enable us to use samples and make estimates (called *statistics*) of the true constants called *parameters* (Gk. *para + metron* = beyond measure) for the populations from which the samples were drawn. In this way we can study the populations themselves. The process is indicated in Fig. 2–1.

i. The population studied must always be regarded as very large or unlimited, even though we are perhaps concerned with a small number of plants subjected to a completely novel treatment so that no other plants of the same sort in fact exist. It must be possible in principle to provide a large population of other similar plants or else the data are not of scientific value for the observations cannot be repeated. Unique observations may be of value as a stimulus to speculation but this in turn is of value only if it leads to experiments.

In science we are always concerned with one, or a very few, of the attributes of the individuals making up a population (p. 1), such as their weight or nitrogen content or some other characteristic that can be

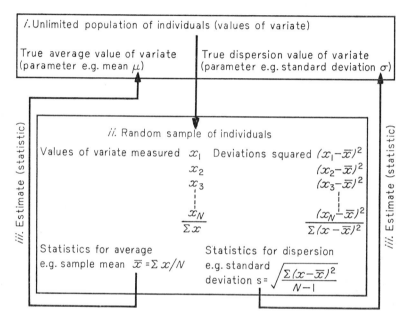

Fig. 2–1   Method of studying a population by means of a sample.

expressed in quantitative terms, even if only on an arbitrary scale. We therefore really study a population of values of an attribute, which because it varies is called a *variate*. We need a few mathematical constants (parameters) which ideally should compress all we want to know about such a population into a few numerical values, easier to grasp than the original bulky data. Especially we need some sort of an average value of the variate, and probably the most generally useful one is the *mean* (μ); also some constant which specifies the variability or *dispersion* of the values and here the *standard deviation* (σ) or its square, the *variance* (σ^2), is generally used. It must be emphasized that measures of variability are at least as important in characterizing a population as average values. Consider the effects on the profits of a chain store selling trousers if they knew the average length of leg of the male population but had no information on the relative numbers of men with various leg lengths.

ii. Such 'true' constants (denoted by Greek letters) can never be known exactly but can be estimated as statistics (denoted by italic letters) calculated from samples with an accuracy that increases with sample size.

The only way to obtain a representative sample from a population is to take a *random sample*, which may be defined as one so chosen as to give each individual in the population an equal and *independent* chance of being chosen. This can only be achieved by the use of some physical apparatus such as dice, roulette wheels or playing cards, or else specially prepared tables of random numbers; it is impossible to avoid unconscious bias in trying to think of 'random' numbers, or in deciding to choose 'this plant, that one and the one over there'. Even worse, any attempt to choose 'average' individuals not only assumes that we know the average value that we wish to determine, and ensures that we cannot find it, but prevents us from obtaining any information about variability.

If we may not 'choose' individuals, except by some such process as giving each one a different number and then taking random numbers, what may we do in the way of discarding unsatisfactory individuals when they are indicated by the randomizing process? That depends on how we define the population we wish to study. If it is the whole population, no individual must be discarded. Thus if we were studying the yield of fresh weight of radishes per basin or per unit area by taking samples, we should include any missing plants as of zero weight in calculating the mean sample weight. If we were interested in the weight per living plant any gaps should be omitted from the samples and if we were only studying plants free from disease, any plants seen to be diseased must be discarded and others (again chosen at random) taken instead. Such omission of unsatisfactory plants must *not* be based on inspection of the values of the variate measured: if they appear to be diseased they must be discarded, whatever their size; if there are no obvious symptoms of disease or damage they must be included however small (e.g. the plant in the 4th row of basin II which weighed less than 0·05 g). It is however permissible, and may be valuable in detecting errors, to re-examine and re-weigh plants recorded as *excessively* small or large, if they are still available. The decision as to what constitutes 'obvious symptoms of disease or damage', as with all other qualitative classifications, may be a difficult one: if we interpret it too widely and discard all thin and weakly plants we shall not have a representative sample of a population subject to competition but some undefined mixture of the more successful competitors. However, the rule that values must not be discarded as 'bad' ones simply from inspection of the data should be absolute. The most that is permissible is to present the results as calculated both with and without the 'bad' values; these may well only represent some of the more extreme effects of random variation and as such give a valuable indication of the possible range.

We now see that by deliberately choosing the two middle rows of basin II for our hypothetical gibberellic acid experiment we should deny the chance of being chosen to plants showing more extreme random variation, namely those weighing less than 2·2 g or more than 12·8 g on 25–6th March (Table I). We should therefore be more likely to detect a real effect of the treatments (if such existed) but the results would not necessarily apply to the whole of the available population of 'inner' plants. A method of combining these two *desiderata* is discussed in Chapter 3.

2.3 Systematic variation in the material

When we can perceive a pattern in the variation among individuals it is an indication of non-random or 'systematic' variation and we usually interpret the pattern as due to one or a few causes whose effects are large compared with the other sources of variation, which we consider to be 'random' causes. For example, the generally smaller weight of the inner plants (mean 5·80 g) than the edge plants (mean 9·63 g) has been interpreted as due to competition for light. We could decide to ignore this and treat all the plants as belonging to one population, as we should if we were studying yield per basin, and our random sampling would give both edge and inner plants equal chances of being chosen, in due proportions. Alternatively we could separate them and treat them as belonging to two populations, or confine our attention to the inner plants as being subjected to competition on all sides. Here the clue was obtained from inspection of the data but all the edge plants whether large or small would be discarded as a class for an apparently good theoretical reason—this is quite different from discarding individual 'bad' values. Similarly we could treat a group of people or animals of two sexes as belonging to one population, or to two separate populations, or we could study one sex only.

Sometimes systematic variation is continuous rather than discontinuous. If our radishes had been grown in a sloping garden bed there might be a gradient of fertility from top to bottom, so that on the whole the plants tended to increase continuously in size down the bed. Again we could ignore this and take random samples over the whole bed; or we might divide it into strips running at right angles to the direction of the gradient and so have representatives of a number of populations of radishes of different mean size, each with less variability (smaller dispersion) than for the bed as a whole. A group of animals or people of various ages could again be treated as members of one population or could be divided into age groups.

2.4 Random variation in measurement ('noise')

If we were to weigh a steel ball-bearing over and over again, on an automatic recording balance so as to avoid being influenced by previous results, we should find that the successive records showed a certain amount of variation; for example, with a rather poor 'three-place balance': 1·002, 0·999, 1·000, 0·998. . . . In this way we could build up a population of measurements of weight in which the variation was entirely due to random variation in the method of measurement (called 'noise' in electronics) for it could be assumed that, unlike a radish plant, the ball would in fact remain of virtually constant weight, to much finer limits than indicated by the weighings. We see therefore that the random variation ordinarily found, for instance in the fresh weights of radish plants, is made up of two parts which can never be completely separated: *a* 'noise' and *b* random variation in the material itself. The measurements should be accurate enough for the 'noise' to be much smaller than the random variation in the material, for only so can the latter be estimated, but it is usually a waste of time and effort to make it many orders of magnitude smaller. In biology it is seldom worth while to weigh or measure to a greater accuracy than 1 per cent of the value for the smaller individuals in the sample. The usual practice is to measure heights of men to the nearest $\frac{1}{10}$ in. (2·5 mm), but much more information could be obtained about a population by measuring to the nearest $\frac{1}{2}$ in. only (or, say, to 1 cm) and using the time saved to deal with a larger sample.

2.5   Systematic variation in measurement

The word 'errors' is often, and I think regrettably, used to mean random variation, which is not erroneous but an aspect of nature; here however we are concerned with errors due to faulty technique and *systematic errors* is an appropriate term. For example, many measuring instruments depend in principle on changes of electrical resistance; these are often sensitive to temperature and if a suitable correction is not made the same value of a variate may give different readings at different seasons or times of day. Again, with a simple beam balance one of the weights may have been damaged and weigh much less than it should. This will result in all weighings in which it is included giving gross overestimates. This example shows that systematic errors merge into random variation as they are reduced in magnitude. None of the weights can be exactly correct and their positive or negative deviations from their nominal values contribute to the random variation in weighings made with the balance. It is only when the deviation for one weight is very large compared with those for the others that it leads to systematic errors, nor will these be important if they are very small relative to the random variation in the material. Similarly, in the first example, a temperature correction would not be worth while if its effect was small compared with the other sources of variation.

2.6   Study of variation by frequency distributions

The first step in studying the variation in a population is to take a large sample, preferably of more than 100 individuals, and tabulate the measurements made in a *frequency table*. The observed range of the variate is divided into a number of classes and the number of individuals (frequency) falling in each class recorded. This can be done by making a mark in the appropriate box of the table for each measurement and then counting the marks. Any observation falling exactly between two classes is allotted as a half to each. To illustrate the information given in a frequency table a *frequency diagram* should be drawn; the best type is called a *histogram* in which the classes are marked off along a horizontal line and a column of *area* proportional to the frequency is erected above each class interval.

If the variate is *discrete*, changing by whole numbers only as do the numbers of petals in flowers or the numbers of animals in litters, the successive classes should increase by the same units as the variate. For a *continuous* variate, such as weight or height, the range should be divided into 10 to 20 classes, or rather fewer for samples of less than 100 or for very irregular data. If the more extreme classes are found to contain very few individuals they may be made wider and in a histogram the area (not the height) of the column must still be made proportional to the frequency.

For taking very large samples in the field it may be convenient to collect the data directly as frequencies; this involves deciding on the class intervals first on the basis of preliminary sampling.

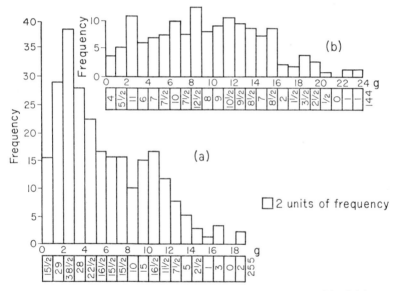

Fig. 2–2 Frequency tables and histograms for fresh weights (g) of (a) 255 'inner' radish plants and (b) 144 edge plants (data in Table 1).

Frequency histograms for the fresh weights of the 255 inner and 144 edge plants are shown in Fig. 2–2 (a) and (b), together with the frequency tables from which they were plotted. The class with the greatest number of individuals is called the *modal class* and for the inner plants this is much further to the left (2–3 g) than for the edge plants (8–9 g), though the latter also have a subsidiary peak at 2–3 g. Perhaps, under conditions of

competition, seedlings which are initially shaded by others fall further and
further behind, tending to reach about this size in 5 weeks; especially for
the inner plants, relatively few very large plants can shade many small
ones (cf. OBEID et al., 1967).

If larger and larger samples are taken from a population the frequency
diagrams become less and less irregular in shape and more and more alike
for successive samples. They tend towards the *frequency distribution of the
unlimited population*. For a discrete variate this must always be step-like
as in a histogram. However, for a continuous variate, the class intervals
could be made narrower and narrower (at least in theory) as the size of
sample was increased, so that ultimately the outline of the histogram would
become a smooth curve, the *frequency curve of the unlimited population*. If
two attributes are measured for the same individuals, the class intervals for
the two variates can be plotted at right angles on a horizontal plane surface
and the frequencies plotted vertically to make a *frequency surface* in three
dimensions; this idea can be extended theoretically to more than two variates
to give a 'multidimensional surface'.

It is essential to grasp the idea of an unlimited population distributed in
some characteristic frequency distribution in respect of the attribute or
attributes measured, for this underlies all statistical work and probably
should underlie all work in any of the sciences; certainly this is true of
biology.

Frequency curves are of many different types. That for the fresh weights
of inner plants would almost certainly be very *skew*, with the *mode* (the
value of the variate corresponding to the maximum frequency) close to
zero and a long tail to the right. If log (fresh weight) is used as the variate
instead of fresh weight itself, the distribution becomes skew the other way
with the mode on the right. The frequency curve for fresh weights of edge
plants might prove to be fairly symmetrical, though there could well be a
long tail on the right while on the left there must be cut off at zero weight;
another possibility is that the curve might have two modes. A bi-modal
frequency curve indicates a mixture in the population of two types due to a
'systematic' or non-random cause (p. 29); for example the curve for a
population of height measurements of both men and women would probably be bi-modal.

The only type of frequency curve that will be discussed here, and that
briefly, is the *normal curve*. More information on the *normal distribution*
for continuous variates, and on the *Poisson* and *binomial* distributions for
discrete variates, should be obtained from text books on statistical methods.

2.6.1   The normal distribution

Fig. 2–3 (a) shows a normal curve. This has the equation

$$y = \frac{N}{\sigma\sqrt{2\pi}}\, e^{-0\cdot5((x-\mu)/\sigma)^2} \tag{2.1}$$

where y is the frequency, x is the variate, N is the total number of observations of x, e is the base of Naperian logarithms ($2 \cdot 71828 \ldots$) and π is $3 \cdot 14159 \ldots$; μ is one of the parameters of the curve, the '*true*' *mean* value of x and coincides with the mode; σ is the other parameter and is called the *standard deviation*, it is in the same units as x and geometrically it specifies the distance on either side of μ to the point of inflection or steepest part of the curve. The maximum value of y is given by $\dfrac{N}{\sigma \sqrt{2\pi}}$ for when $x = \mu$, $x - \mu = 0$ and $\mathrm{e}^{-0 \cdot 5((x-\mu)/\sigma)^2} = \mathrm{e}^0 = 1$. For any other given *deviation* $(x - \mu)$, whether positive or negative, $(x - \mu)^2$ will be positive and e will

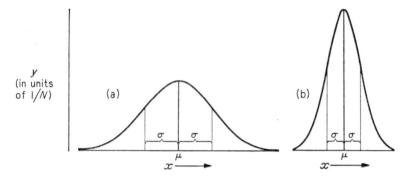

Fig. 2–3 Normal curves with the variate x plotted against relative frequency ($1/N$): (**a**) with large σ (wide dispersion); (**b**) with small σ (small dispersion).

be raised to a negative power. The curve therefore falls symmetrically on either side of the maximum but however large or small x becomes, y will never fall to zero. The theoretical curve in fact extends from $x = -\infty$ to $x = +\infty$ and this is certainly not true of any biological variate! In practice, however, this is not important as the frequency y falls to negligible values at no very great distance from μ.

The two unknown parameters, μ and σ, of the normal curve are estimated from a sample by the statistics $\bar{x}$ and s (Fig. 2–1, iii). $\bar{x}$ is simply the arithmetic mean of all the observed values of x, i.e. $\bar{x} = \dfrac{\sum x}{N}$. The *estimated standard deviation*, $s = \sqrt{\dfrac{\sum (x - \bar{x})^2}{N-1}}$ is the square root of the *estimated variance* (s^2), which is found by dividing the sum of squares of deviations $\sum (x - \bar{x})^2$, called '*sum of squares*' for short, by the number of *degrees of freedom* $n = (N-1)$. There are only $(N-1)$ degrees of freedom available for calculating s^2 because one has been used up in calculating $\bar{x}$ from which the deviations are measured.

The two statistics $\bar{x}$ and s contain between them all the available information about the distribution, assuming it to be normal, from which the sample came. The mean $\bar{x}$ merely estimates the position of the middle of the distribution μ and therefore the shape of the curve depends entirely on the standard deviation σ, estimated by s. The area under the curve can be made constant at unity by using relative instead of absolute frequencies: if each observation is called $1/N$ the total frequency becomes unity. (As in a histogram the area is proportional to the frequency.) We see then (Fig. 2–3 (b)) that a small value of σ gives a tall narrow curve with the values closely grouped round the mean (small 'scatter' or dispersion) while a large σ has the converse effects (Fig. 2–3 (a)).

The importance of the normal distribution lies in there being a better 'tool kit' of statistical methods available for this than for any other type. Some biological variates approximate to the normal distribution sufficiently well for methods based on it to be applied to the unmodified or 'raw' data. This is generally true, for instance, of heights of men or women. Often, however, the distribution is too asymmetrical or differs too much in other ways from the normal and then *transformed data* may be calculated in the hope that they will be more nearly normally distributed. Using log (fresh weight) for the inner plants represented such an attempt but as mentioned above this particular *transformation* over-corrected the skewness of the distribution. A more generally useful method, discussed below, involves planning experiments so that the unit data consist of means or totals of measurements from a number of individuals; these are likely to be more nearly normal in their distribution.

Distribution of means, variances and differences between means. If we take a large number of samples of the same size, say N individual values in each, from a normally distributed population and for each sample calculate the mean $\bar{x}$ and the variance s^2, these statistics will of course be found to vary from sample to sample. For use in tests of significance we need to know their frequency distributions, as will be discussed later. The estimates $\bar{x}$ of the true mean μ for the original normal population will themselves be normally distributed, also with a true mean of μ but with a true variance of σ^2/N; the larger the samples, therefore, the more closely will the values of $\bar{x}$ be grouped around μ (Fig. 2–4 (b) and (c)). If N is a large number the estimates s^2 of the true variance σ^2 for the original normal distribution will also be normally distributed with a true mean of σ^2 and a true variance of $2\sigma^4/(N-1)$; estimates s^2 from small samples are not normally distributed.

If samples of N are taken at random from a normally distributed population as discussed above, grouped in pairs at random and the difference $(\bar{x}_1 - \bar{x}_2)$ between the two means calculated for each pair, these differences will again be found to be normally distributed, with a true mean of zero (for obviously positive and negative differences should average out) and a true variance of $2\sigma^2/N$. This illustrates the rule that the variance of the difference (or sum) of two independent quantities is the sum of their variances, for each of the single means has a variance of σ^2/N.

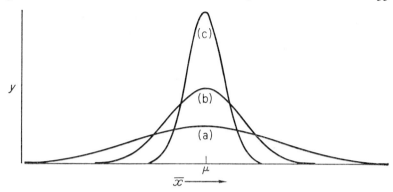

Fig. 2–4 Normal curves: (a) for single values of the variate x, (b) for means $\bar{x}$ of 4 values; (c) for means $\bar{x}$ of 16 values; y is relative frequency.

The best estimates of the variances for means, variances and differences between means are obtained by substituting the value of s^2 calculated from a sample (p. 33) for σ^2 in the expressions given above. The larger the sample the better the estimates will be.

It is most fortunate that even when the distribution of individual values is very far from normal, the distribution of means of N tends towards normality as N is increased: in fact, if N is 4 or more it is fairly safe to assume that the distribution of means (or sums) will be near enough to normal for statistical methods based on the normal distribution to be used. This applies to continuous variates, and even to most discrete variates if the number of *different* individual values is fairly large—say 6 or more which occur reasonably often. As an example, Fig. 2–5 (a) shows a frequency histogram for sums and means calculated for 63 sets of 4 inner plants,

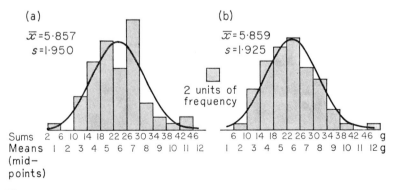

Fig. 2–5 Frequency histograms and fitted normal curves for fresh weights (g) of 'inner' radish plants. (Same data as in Fig. 2–2 (a)). Sums or means of: (a) random sets of 4 plants; (b) sets of 4 adjacent plants in square 'plots'.

taken at random from the 255 individuals shown in Fig. 2–2 (a). A mathematically fitted normal curve superimposed on the histogram shows that there is now little evidence that the data are not normally distributed.

In Fig. 2–5 (b) a similar diagram shows the result of taking groups of 4 adjacent inner plants, in small square 'plots'. The almost identical standard deviation s shows that there was no appreciable systematic variation due to position among the inner plants; if there had been, s would probably have been increased when each set of 4 plants was taken all from one locality. In this particular example, therefore, a set of 2×2 adjacent inner plants chosen at random would have provided as representative a sample as a set of 4 completely random individuals. A similar situation *might* apply if the plants had been grown four to a pot in well mixed soil, though differences in filling the pots and in watering might then increase pot to pot variation, analogous to systematic variation over an area. It certainly would be unsafe to assume such a state of affairs for field or garden plots where systematic variation in soil fertility is general.

Probability. Many books have been written on this subject. Here it will be discussed very briefly and from one view point only.

If all normal curves are reduced to a single standard form, it is possible to tabulate for this curve numerical values which can then be used in all subsequent calculations for normal distributions. The first step was to make all the curves of the same area by using relative frequencies (p. 34). The second step is to plot y against deviations of x from the true mean μ expressed in terms of the standard deviation σ, that is against $(x-\mu)/\sigma$. This gives a single standard normal curve with a central value of zero and unit standard deviation (Fig. 2–6); obviously, when $x=\mu$, $(x-\mu)/\sigma=0$, and when $(x-\mu)=\sigma$, $(x-\mu)/\sigma=1$.

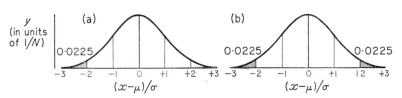

Fig. 2–6 Standard normal curve, with unit area, zero mean and unit standard deviation: (**a**) the probability integral gives the area to the left of a given ordinate, here shown at -2; (**b**) the probability of a positive *or* negative deviation beyond a given pair of ordinates is twice the probability integral.

For this standard curve the area to the left of an ordinate placed at various positions had been calculated and tabulated. This area is called the *probability integral* and gives the total relative frequency below the ordinate in question, that is, the *probability* that an individual chosen at random from a normally distributed population will have a smaller value of $(x-\mu)/\sigma$ than that ordinate. Thus for a value of $(x-\mu)/\sigma$ of -2.0, the probability integral is 0·0225, so that 2·25 per cent of the population will deviate from the mean on the negative side by 2 or more standard deviations; the probability P of a single individual doing so is 0·0225 in 1·0 or about 1 in 44 (Fig. 2–6 (a)).

If we are interested in the probability of a randomly chosen individual having either a positive *or* negative deviation from the mean exceeding a given value, as we usually are, then the values of the probability integral must of course be doubled. In the above example, therefore, there is a 1 in 22 chance of the individual having a deviation outside the limits $\mu \pm 2\sigma$ and P now has the value 0·045 because both tails of the curve are included (Fig. 2–6 (b)). Such values of twice the probability integral are tabulated by FISHER and YATES (1963, Table 1) and some representative values are shown here in Table 2.

Table 2 Values of probability P corresponding to the normal deviate $d = \pm (x - \mu)/\sigma$; P gives the relative area for two tails of the normal curve. (From Table I, Fisher, R.A. and Yates, F. (1963). *Statistical Tables for Biological, Agricultural and Medical Research*. 6th ed. Oliver and Boyd, Edinburgh, by permission of the authors and publishers)

d	0·99	1·64	1·96	2·58	3·29	6·11
P	0·320	0·10	0·05	0·010	0·001	0·000 000 001

Thirty-two per cent of the observations will fall outside the range $\mu \pm \sigma$, 1% outside the range $\mu \pm 2\cdot6\sigma$, one in a thousand outside $\mu \pm 3\cdot3\sigma$, while an individual taken at random would only fall outside the range $\mu \pm 6\cdot1\sigma$ once in a thousand million trials. As noted above (p. 33) the extent of the normal curve from minus infinity to plus infinity is without practical importance.

2.7   Confidence limits and tests of significance

Probabilities obtained from the standard normal curve as just discussed may be used for any normally distributed values, whether these are observations (x) on single individuals, means of N observations ($\bar{x}$), differences between random pairs of means ($\bar{x}_1 - \bar{x}_2$), or (for large samples only) estimated variances (s^2). However, in order to obtain them we have to substitute σ by an estimate s and this is only satisfactory if the latter is based on at least 30 degrees of freedom (p. 33).

Tests of significance. The standard deviation of a distribution of means, differences between means, or indeed of anything except single observations, is, for no very good reason, called a *standard error*. If the standard error for a distribution of means $\bar{x}$ is estimated as $E_{\bar{x}} = s/\sqrt{N}$ (p. 34) and s is calculated from a large sample, a deviation from the true mean μ of

$\pm 2E_{\bar{x}}$ or more should occur only once in 22 trials, that is, $P = 0.045$. This probability, or more usually P0·05 which corresponds to a deviation of *about* twice the standard error (Table 2), is taken as the conventional limit in judging whether a deviation is *significant* or not (Fig. 2–7). If an observed

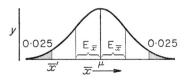

Fig. 2–7   Normal distribution of means ($\bar{x}$) of N observations, with estimated standard error $E_{\bar{x}}$. An observed value $\bar{x}'$ is shown $-1.96E_{\bar{x}}$ away from the hypothetical true mean μ. The probability of a positive *or* negative deviation as large as, or larger than, this is P0·05.

mean $\bar{x}$ lies more than $\pm 1.96E_{\bar{x}}$ away from a hypothetical true value μ (often zero) we conclude that it probably does not belong to a population distributed about that value, and that the hypothesis is disproved with $P < 0.05$; it may still be true but only if a rather improbable event has occurred, such as would be expected in less than one trial in every 20. If we are not satisfied with this we may set the limits at $\pm 2.6E_{\bar{x}}$ (P0·01) and then the hypothesis will be rejected when it is in fact true less than once in 100 trials. These conventional levels of P are arbitrary and we may take any other level we consider sufficiently safe, as long as we state it—we can never achieve certainty. A value $(\bar{x} - \mu)/E_{\bar{x}}$ greater than $+1.6$ or less than -1.6 should lead us to suspect our hypothetical value for μ, for such a large deviation would be expected in less than 1 trial in 10 if μ were correct (Table 2); although not considered to disprove the hypothesis, a value of $P < 0.1$ indicates the need for further investigation.

Confidence limits. Note that the value we use for μ is always fixed by hypothesis, not calculated from the data, and it does not therefore involve a degree of freedom. However, instead of testing whether our observed $\bar{x}$ shows a significant deviation from a hypothetical value μ, that we have arrived at on theoretical grounds, we may accept $\bar{x}$ as the best available estimate of an unspecified μ and calculate the *confidence limits* within which μ may be expected to lie with a stated probability. If we try different values of μ we shall find that $\bar{x}$ is significantly different from μ whenever $(\bar{x} - \mu)/E_{\bar{x}}$ exceeds $+1.96$ or is less than -1.96 (Fig. 2–7), so we can say that the sample shows significant aberration, with a probability of P0·05, from any population with a true mean μ outside the limits $\bar{x} \pm 1.96E_{\bar{x}}$. Conversely, the true mean μ is likely, with a probability of P0·95 or 19 in 20, to lie within these confidence limits; again, on the average, this supposition will be wrong once in 20 trials. The importance for many practical purposes of being able to place confidence limits on an estimated mean is obvious. Experiments are often carried out to estimate the magnitude of an effect that in qualitative terms is well known, for example to estimate the responses of a crop to different dressings of a nitrogenous fertilizer in a particular situation in order to decide what is likely to be an economic rate of application. Confidence limits are important as a basis for such a decision; they also provide the test of significance, for if they span zero the effect is non-significant.

Since the variance of the mean $\bar{x}$ is s^2/N, it can be reduced by increasing the sample size, which does not systematically affect the values of either $\bar{x}$ or the variance s^2 for single observations. Having calculated $\bar{x}$, s^2 and confidence limits $\bar{x} \pm 1.96s/\sqrt{N}$ from a sample we can estimate the sample size needed to give any other desired confidence limits:

if $D = \pm 1.96s/\sqrt{N}$ is the desired deviation from $\bar{x}$ for 95 per cent confidence limits, $N = 3.84s^2/D^2$. To halve D, the sample size must be multiplied by four.

Confidence limits may be calculated not only for means $\bar{x}$ but also for the other statistics mentioned in the first paragraph of this section— $(\bar{x}_1 - \bar{x}_2)$ or s^2.

Experiment with two large samples ($N_1 > 30$, $N_2 > 30$). In experimental work in biology we are seldom able to use large enough samples to be able to test whether the values of the variate for single individuals are normally distributed and it is not often safe to assume this, though the assumption is generally made. For example, the calculations mentioned on p. 25 were made on the assumption that the fresh weights of the 16 radish plants belonged to a normal population; Fig. 2–2 (a) shows clearly that they did not, and the chances given are therefore of doubtful validity, though the general conclusion is not in doubt. If we arrange for our unit data (x) to be totals or means for a constant number of 4 or more individuals these may generally be assumed to be normally distributed (p. 35). With this knowledge we can design a better experiment to compare fresh weight growth in the GA and (1) treatments. The four basins of radish plants (Table 1) provided 64 square plots, each of 4 inner plants, except for one missing plant to which we may allot the mean weight for the other three in the 'plot' without much loss of accuracy. We could number these plots 1 to 64 and allot the GA treatment to the first 32 numbers between 1 and 64 looked up in a table of random numbers, the rest having (1), or we could use one of the other methods of randomizing mentioned on p. 23. Two series of plot totals obtained in this way, denoted by x_{GA} and $x_{(1)}$, are shown in Table 3, together with the 'treatment' totals and the 'treatment' means. We want to know whether the difference between the two 'treatment' means $(\bar{x}_{GA} - \bar{x}_{(1)})$ is such as would be unlikely to arise in two independent samples from a single normally distributed population by random variation

Table 3 Experiment with two large samples ($N_1 > 30$, $N_2 > 30$). Fresh weights (g) per plot of 4 radish plants, allotted to 2 fictitious treatments supposed applied 21 days before harvest: d tests of significance of difference of two means; also confidence limits.

x_{GA}	$x_{(1)}$
22·9	21·2
30·0	25·0
26·2	15·2
15·9	20·8
19·5	15·2
33·9	11·4
34·5	25·4
27·4	22·1
24·6	26·6
21·9	38·7
22·9	30·8
23·4	22·4
18·4	20·2
27·8	23·4
26·0	14·1
21·5	15·7
30·4	26·9
18·5	14·4
29·7	10·7
18·3	25·2
16·6	13·2
16·3	13·2
16·4	26·5
27·7	33·5
8·6	46·6
20·8	32·1
34·5	32·9
12·6	36·6
19·9	25·7
10·6	17·8
19·2	25·5
33·7	23·7
$\sum x_{GA} = 730·6$	$\sum x_{(1)} = 752·7$
$\bar{x}_{GA} = 22·831$ g	$\bar{x}_{(1)} = 23·522$ g

d test for means and confidence limits

$s_{GA}^2 = \sum (x_{GA} - \bar{x}_{GA})^2 \div (N_{GA} - 1)$
$= \{\sum x_{GA}^2 - (\sum x_{GA})^2 / N_{GA}\} \div (N_{GA} - 1)$
$= \{18169·72 - 533776·36/32\} \div 31$
$= 48·039$

where $(\sum x_{GA})^2 / N_{GA}$ is the correction for an assumed mean of zero.

$s_{(1)}^2 = 72·613$

$E_{(\bar{x}_{GA} - \bar{x}_{(1)})} = \sqrt{(s_{GA}^2 / N_{GA}) + (s_{(1)}^2 / N_{(1)})}$
$= 1·942$ g

$d = \{(\bar{x}_{GA} - \bar{x}_{(1)}) - 0\} \div E_{(\bar{x}_{GA} - \bar{x}_{(1)})}$
$= -0·691/1·942 = -0·356$

$P = 0·72$

Confidence limits for $(\bar{x}_{GA} - \bar{x}_{(1)})$ for $P0·05$
$= (\bar{x}_{GA} - \bar{x}_{(1)}) \pm d_{.05} E_{(\bar{x}_{GA} - \bar{x}_{(1)})}$

where $d_{.05}$ is the value of d for $P0·05$
$= -0·69 \pm 1·96 \times 1·94$
$= -4·49$ and $+3·11$ g

alone. We make the zero hypothesis that the two series of 32 values do in fact belong to the same population, so that the true difference between the means is zero (p. 34), and we ask the above question in more precise terms: 'What is the probability of a negative or positive difference as large as or larger than $(\bar{x}_{GA} - \bar{x}_{(1)})$ occurring in a population of differences between random pairs of means for 32 plots, normally distributed about a true mean difference of zero with a standard error of $\sqrt{2\sigma^2/32}$?' If we reject the zero hypothesis on the basis of our observed difference we must also have been willing to do so had we obtained a more extreme deviation from zero. We therefore calculate the probability of a difference 'as large as or larger than' that observed (pp. 12 and 20). Although the difference $(\bar{x}_{GA} - \bar{x}_{(1)})$ that we have found experimentally is negative, we should have been equally concerned to know if it was likely to be a real treatment effect had it been positive. Experience would in fact have led us to expect this but the possibility that GA might really reduce growth could not be ruled out. A very large difference, improbable on the zero hypothesis, would thus be considered to disprove the latter and support a real treatment effect in whichever direction it occurred; we must therefore use both tails of the normal curve to estimate probabilities (a 'two-tailed test').

To obtain the appropriate probability from the table based on the standard normal curve (Table 2; or FISHER and YATES, 1963, Table I) we need to calculate $d = \pm (x - \mu)/\sigma$, but where x is replaced by $(\bar{x}_{GA} - \bar{x}_{(1)})$, and μ by zero; σ should be replaced by the true standard error for the difference between means, $\sqrt{2\sigma^2/N}$, or, if σ_{GA}^2/N_{GA} is the true variance for one mean and $\sigma_{(1)}^2/N_{(1)}$ that for the other, σ should be replaced by $\sqrt{(\sigma_{GA}^2/N_{GA}) + (\sigma^2_{(1)}/N_{(1)})}$ (p. 34). Unfortunately σ_{GA}^2 and $\sigma_{(1)}^2$ are unknown so we substitute s_{GA}^2 and $s_{(1)}^2$; these are each based on 31 degrees of freedom which counts as a large number, so σ^2 can be replaced by s^2 without serious loss of accuracy and with no allowance for the fact that such estimates are subject to random variation (p. 34).

The calculations are shown in Table 3. The procedure for finding the sum of squares for GA, indicated in the first line, would be extremely tedious: 22·83 would have to be subtracted from each value of x_{GA} in turn and the deviations squared and summed. Fortunately the arithmetic can be lightened by using a more convenient 'assumed mean', M, instead of the actual mean $\bar{x}$, and then applying a correction:

$$\sum (x - \bar{x})^2 = \sum (x - M)^2 - \frac{(\sum x - NM)^2}{N}$$

Correct sum of squares	Crude sum of squares	Correction term

If $M = 0$, this reduces to:

$$\sum (x - \bar{x})^2 = \sum x^2 - \frac{(\sum x)^2}{N}$$

If a calculating machine is not available, M should be a round number near to $\bar{x}$; 20 would be suitable for both treatments in Table 3. The squaring should then be done with a table of squares (FISHER and YATES, 1963, LINDLEY and MILLER, 1964, or for 4-figure numbers, BARLOW, 1941) and all squares should be taken out to the full number of figures. For machine calculation it is better to take $M = 0$, as in Table 3. Correction terms should be calculated to the same number of figures as there are in the crude sums of squares. The estimated variances s^2_{GA} and $s^2_{(1)}$ are for the distributions of x_{GA} and $x_{(1)}$ respectively, i.e. of totals for 4 plants; dividing by N_{GA} and $N_{(1)}$ (32 in each case) yields the estimated variances for distributions of means of 32 values ($\bar{x}_{\mathrm{GA}}$ and $\bar{x}_{(1)}$) and adding these gives the estimated variance for the distribution of differences between such means ($\bar{x}_{\mathrm{GA}} - \bar{x}_{(1)}$). The standard error $E_{(\bar{x}_{\mathrm{GA}} - \bar{x}_{(1)})}$ is then obtained by taking the square root and d is calculated as indicated above. The value found for d corresponds to $P = 0.72$, so that a difference from zero in either direction as large as or larger than that observed would be expected in 72 per cent of trials for random pairs of means from a single normal population. Obviously this is consistent with the zero hypothesis; had P been less than 0.05 (1 in 20) we should probably have called the difference 'significant' and if it had been less than 0.01 (1 in 100), 'highly significant', with the zero hypothesis disproved at those levels.

In an example like the present one, it would suffice to inspect the two columns of figures, or to plot them in two frequency histograms, to be satisfied that there was no appreciable effect of the treatments. The only statements that can be made about a non-significant treatment effect are in terms of confidence limits, which are also shown in Table 3 and span zero. They show that the true mean difference probably (P0.95) lay between -4.49 g and $+3.11$ g i.e. that it was either zero or very small and of unknown sign.

2.7.1   Small samples

In most biological experiments the number of degrees of freedom available for calculating the random variance s^2, used in testing the significance of treatment effects, is less than 30 and often very much less; the random variation in the estimates s^2 then becomes important and has to be allowed for.

The distribution of t. Suppose a number of values $\bar{x}$ to be the means of random samples of N drawn from a normal population and $\sigma/\sqrt{N}$ to be their true standard error (p. 34). If $(\bar{x} - \mu)$ is the deviation from the population mean μ, $(\bar{x} - \mu) \div \sigma/\sqrt{N}$ will be normally distributed with unit standard deviation (p. 36). This would be so for any size of sample, but when σ is replaced by s the distribution of $(\bar{x} - \mu) \div s/\sqrt{N}$ is *not* normal if s is based on a small number of degrees of freedom. The frequency distribution has been calculated for this quantity

$$ t = (\bar{x} - \mu) \div \frac{s}{\sqrt{N}} $$

or in words: 'deviation from hypothesis/*estimate* of standard error'.

The shape of the frequency curve for t depends on the number of degrees of freedom n available for calculating s but is independent of σ the true standard deviation. Values of t and corresponding probabilities P, for any number of degrees of freedom n from 1 to 30, are tabulated in most statistical text books or books of tables. The values of P tabulated give the probability of t falling outside the range $\pm t'$, that is for positive *or* negative deviations from the hypothesis, so that both tails of the appropriate t distribution are used (Fig. 2–8). For large samples ($n \simeq \infty$), the t distribution is normal ($s \simeq \sigma$), so that when t is 1·96, P is 0·05 (Table 2). Values of t corresponding to this conventional level of significance, for some other numbers of degrees of freedom n, are given in Table 4. These show that as

Table 4 Values of t, for a probability of P·05, from t distributions for n degrees of freedom. (From Table III, Fisher, R. A. and Yates, F. (1963). *Statistical Tables for Biological, Agricultural and Medical Research.* 6th ed. Oliver and Boyd, Edinburgh, by permission of the authors and publishers)

n	∞	30	15	10	5	2	1
t	1·96	2·04	2·13	2·23	2·57	4·30	12·71

n is decreased the t distribution becomes flatter and wider, with the two tail portions, each $2\frac{1}{2}$ per cent of the total area, lying beyond more and more widely spaced ordinates. If our sample mean $\bar{x}$ were based on only two observations ($n = N - 1 = 1$), a deviation exceeding $\pm 12·7$ times the estimated standard error might be expected to arise from random variation within the population once in every 20 trials. This shows the great uncertainty of s as an estimate of σ under these circumstances. Instead of saying the true mean probably lay within $\bar{x} \pm 2E_{\bar{x}}$ we should have to put the limits as wide as $\bar{x} \pm 12·7E_{\bar{x}}$.

Probabilities from the appropriate t distribution can be used for differences between random pairs of means for small samples, just as the standard normal curve can be used when they are based on large ones, but with degrees of freedom in short supply we make a single combined estimate s^2 of σ^2; this is justified, for by hypothesis the two samples come from the same population. We pool the sums of squares, calculated for each sample separately, and divide by the sum of the degrees of freedom contributed by each i.e.

$$s^2 = \frac{\sum (x_1 - \bar{x}_1)^2 + \sum (x_2 - \bar{x}_2)^2}{(N_1 - 1) + (N_2 - 1)} \qquad (2.2)$$

Note that two constants ($\bar{x}_1$ and $\bar{x}_2$) have been calculated from the data and used to fix the points from which the deviations are measured; this is why the total degrees of freedom (n) for s^2 number $N_1 + N_2 - 2$.

If σ^2 were the true variance for single observations, the variances of the two sample means would be σ^2/N_1 and σ^2/N_2 respectively; the true variance of the difference ($\bar{x}_1 - \bar{x}_2$) would be the sum of the two variances (p. 34): $\sigma^2(1/N_1 + 1/N_2) = \sigma^2(N_1 + N_2)/N_1N_2$. This is $2\sigma^2/N$ if $N_1 = N_2 = N$. Our estimate of the standard error of the difference is

$$E_{(\bar{x}_1 - \bar{x}_2)} = \sqrt{\frac{s^2(N_1 + N_2)}{N_1N_2}} \qquad (2.3)$$

and

$$t = \frac{(\bar{x}_1 - \bar{x}_2) - \mu}{E_{(\bar{x}_1 - \bar{x}_2)}}$$

The zero hypothesis states that μ is zero.

In this method a difference in the variances for the two samples may enhance the value of *t*. A significantly large value of *t* indicates that the samples belong to different populations, but part of the difference could lie in the variances rather than in the means. The variances may be compared separately by the F test (see below) and if they are found significantly different, allowance may be made for this (BAILEY, 1959, section 6.5; COCHRAN and COX, 1957, section 4.14).

As an example of this use of *t* we will assume that the GA (1) experiment was carried out with only one basin of plants (I), the 'treatments' being allotted randomly to the 16 plots, each of 4 inner plants. The data from this supposed experiment and the calculations are shown in Table 5A. The sums of squares have been calculated as in Table 3, using 'assumed means' of zero (p. 41). The value of s^2 obtained (equation **2.2**) is inserted in equation **2.3** to give the estimated standard error ($E_{(\bar{x}_{GA} - \bar{x}_{(1)})}$) for a

Table 5 Experiment with two small samples. Fresh weights (g) per plot of 4 radish plants, allotted 2 fictitious treatments supposed applied 21 days before harvest.

---

*A **t** test for significance of difference of means*

x_{GA}	$x_{(1)}$	
16·6	27·8	$s^2 = \{\sum (x_{GA} - \bar{x}_{GA})^2 + \sum (x_{(1)} - \bar{x}_{(1)})^2\}$
30·4	25·2	$\qquad \div \{(N_{GA} - 1) + (N_{(1)} - 1)\}$
33·5	26·0	$= [\{\sum x_{GA}^2 - (\sum x_{GA})^2 / N_{GA}\}$
29·7	18·3	$\qquad + \{\sum x_{(1)}^2 - (\sum x_{(1)})^2 / N_{(1)}\}]$
13·2	13·2	$\qquad \div \{(N_{GA} - 1) + (N_{(1)} - 1)\}$
46·6	26·5	$= \{(6354·36 - 44100·00/8)$
18·5	16·3	$\qquad + (3829·91 - 28798·09/8)\}$
21·5	16·4	$\qquad \div 14$
$\sum x_{GA} = 210·0$	$\sum x_{(1)} = 169·7$	$= (841·86 + 230·15)/14 = 76·57$
		$E_{(\bar{x}_{GA} - \bar{x}_{(1)})} = \sqrt{s^2(N_{GA} + N_{(1)})/N_{GA}N_{(1)}}$
		$\qquad = \sqrt{76·57 \times 2/8} = 4·375$ g
$\bar{x}_{GA} = 26·250$ g	$\bar{x}_{(1)} = 21·2125$ g	$t = \{(\bar{x}_{GA} - \bar{x}_{(1)}) - 0\} \div E_{(\bar{x}_{GA} - \bar{x}_{(1)})}$
		$\qquad = +5·038/4·375 = +1·1515$
		$n = 14$
		$P > 0·20$ (about 0·25)

B F test for variances

$s_{GA}^2 = 841·86/7 \quad = 120·27; \ n_{GA} = 7$

$s_{(1)}^2 = 230·15/7 \quad = 32·88; \ n_{(1)} = 7$

$F = 120·27/32·88 = \quad 3·66; \ P > 2 \times 0·05$

$\qquad\qquad\qquad$ (5% point F is 3·79 for $n_1 = 7, n_2 = 7$; Table 6B)

C   Analysis of variance

Variation	Degrees of freedom	Sum of squares	Variance	F	F required for P = 0·20
Between treatments	1	101·50*	101·50	1·326 = t^2	1·81
Within treatments	14	(841·86 + 230·15)	76·57		
Total	15	1173·51	—		

*In the special case when $N_T = 2$,

$$N_R \sum (\bar{x}_T - \bar{x})^2 = N_R\{(\bar{x}_{GA} - \bar{x})^2 + (\bar{x}_{(1)} - \bar{x})^2\} \quad (\text{pp. } 48\text{–}9)$$
$$= 8\{(\bar{x}_{GA} - \bar{x}_{(1)})/2\}^2 . 2 = (\bar{x}_{GA} - \bar{x}_{(1)})^2 . 16/4$$
$$= 4(5\cdot038)^2 = 101\cdot50$$

distribution of differences between means of 8 plots. t is found to be $+1\cdot15$ corresponding to a value of P of about 0·25, i.e. a value of t greater than this, *or* less than $-1\cdot15$, would be expected in about 25 per cent of similar experiments where the two samples were drawn from a single normal population. The zero hypothesis is therefore supported. The theoretical procedures underlying the test of significance in this experiment are shown in Fig. 2–8. If there were a good theoretical reason for believing that a real

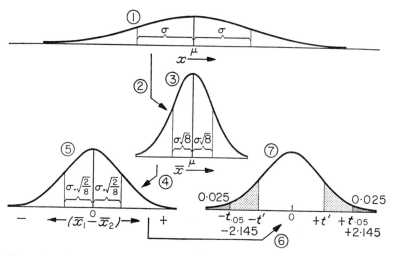

Fig. 2–8   Theoretical procedure in an experiment with two small samples ① Normal distribution of individual plot totals x (4 plants each). ② Samples taken, each of 8 plot totals. ③ Normal distribution of means $\bar{x}$ of 8 plot totals. ④ Samples taken in random pairs. ⑤ Normal distribution of differences $\bar{x}_1 - \bar{x}_2$ between pairs of means. ⑥ One sample difference has an estimate s of σ based on only $7+7$ degrees of freedom. ⑦ Distribution of t for 14 degrees of freedom; the observed value $+t'$ (or an equal negative value $-t'$) gives a probability P of about 0·25; t would have to reach $\pm 2\cdot145$ for a significance of P0·05.

treatment effect could only occur in one direction (say a positive value of $\bar{x}_{GA} - \bar{x}_{(1)}$) then we should carry out a 'one-tailed test' and halve the probability found from the table of t, so that P0·25 would become P0·125 and P0·10 would become P0·05; an apparently 'significant' deviation in the other direction would then be attributed to chance.

The distribution of the variance ratio F. If we wish to test whether one treatment has significantly increased variability compared with the other we cannot use t, which depends upon the deviation tested being normally distributed, though with an unknown true standard error. As values of s^2 from small samples are not normally distributed another frequency distribution has to be used. This is the distribution of $F = s_1^2/s_2^2$, where s_1^2 and s_2^2 are based upon n_1 and n_2 degrees of freedom. F is tabulated with the convention that $s_1^2 > s_2^2$ and is always therefore made greater than unity; n_1 corresponds to the larger variance and n_2 to the smaller. A few values of F for two levels of probability P are shown in Table 6. The probabilities in

Table 6   (From Tables 7 (a) and (b), Lindley, D. V. and Miller, J. C. P. (1964). *Cambridge Elementary Statistical Tables.* Cambridge University Press, London, by permission of the authors and publishers)

A $2\frac{1}{2}\%$ points (P0·025) for the variance ratio (F) distribution

n_1	I	7	24	∞
n_2				
I	648	948	997	1018
7	8·07	4·99	4·42	4·14
24	5·72	2·87	2·27	1·94
∞	5·02	2·29	1·64	1·00

B 5% points (P0·05)

1	161·4	236·8	249·0	254·3
7	5·59	3·79	3·41	3·23
14	4·60	2·76	2·35	2·13
24	4·26	2·42	1·98	1·73
∞	3·84	2·01	1·52	1·00

tables of F are for one tail only and give the chances of F exceeding the tabulated value. For the present purpose, however, we wish to test whether *either* variance is the greater, for either treatment might cause greater variability than the other, so that we need a two-tailed test. Because of the way the tables are prepared it is more convenient to interchange n_{GA} and $n_{(1)}$, making two one-tailed tests, one for $s_{GA}^2 > s_{(1)}^2$ ($n_{GA} = n_1$) and the other for $s_{(1)}^2 > s_{GA}^2$ ($n_{(1)} = n_1$), instead of calculating $s_{GA}^2/s_{(1)}^2$ when $s_{GA}^2 < s_{(1)}^2$ for F would then be less than unity. If the two samples are of the same size ($n_1 = n_2$) as in the present example the F distribution is symmetrical and F is of course unaffected by interchanging the degrees of freedom as above; we can then simply use the values from the $2\frac{1}{2}$ per cent table of F as equivalent to P0·05, or 5 per cent to P0·10 (Table 5B). If the two samples are of unequal size ($n_1 \neq n_2$) the F distribution is skew so that in a two-tailed test the equal areas (probabilities) would be cut off by ordinates at different distances from the centre. We see from Table 6A that if $n_a = 7$ and $n_b = 24$ a value of $F = s_a^2/s_b^2$ greater than 2·87 (when $s_a^2 > s_b^2$) or a value of $F = s_b^2/s_a^2$ greater than 4·42 (when $s_b^2 > s_a^2$) would occur owing to random variation alone within a single normally distributed population once in 20 trials (P0·05).

In Table 5B the variances, s_{GA}^2 and $s_{(1)}^2$, have been calculated separately for each 'treatment', using the sums of squares already obtained in Table 5A. Because $s_{GA}^2 > s_{(1)}^2$, F has been calculated as $s_{GA}^2/s_{(1)}^2$ and found to be 3·66. Table 6B shows that for $n_1 = 7$ and $n_2 = 7$ a value of $F = s_{GA}^2/s_{(1)}^2$ greater than 3·79 would be expected in 5 per cent of experiments, if the two samples in fact came from a single population. However, of such experiments another 5 per cent would be expected to give $F = s_{(1)}^2/s_{GA}^2$ greater than 3·79. The combined probability for $F = 3·66$ is therefore P > 0·1 and the zero hypothesis, that 'treatment' has been without effect on variability, is supported.

Equivalence of tests of significance. In the *t* test, the statistic

$$t = \sqrt{\frac{(\bar{x}-\mu)^2}{1}} \Big/ \sqrt{\frac{1}{N} \cdot \frac{\sum (x-\bar{x})^2}{N-1}} \quad \text{(p. 42)}$$

is in fact the ratio of two standard deviations: the first based on a single deviation ($\bar{x} - \mu$) from a hypothetical value μ and thence having one degree of freedom; the second based on N deviations from a calculated value $\bar{x}$ and having $N-1$ degrees of freedom. If we square *t* we have therefore a variance ratio with $n_1 = 1$ and $n_2 = N-1$, that is $t^2 = F = \{(\bar{x}-\mu)^2/1\} \div s^2/N$. Similarly, the normal deviate d for the standard normal curve (p. 41) is also equivalent to F, but with $n_1 = 1$ and $n_2 = \infty$, for $d^2 = \{(\bar{x}-\mu)^2/1\} \div \sigma^2$ and the true variance σ^2 is based on an infinite number of degrees of freedom. The equivalence of these three tests is indicated in Table 7. The χ^2 test is

Table 7 Equivalence of d, t and F at P0·05 with $n_1 = 1$.

n_2	d	d^2	t	t^2	F
5	—	—	2·57	6·61	6·61
12	—	—	2·18	4·75	4·75
∞	1·96	3·84	1·96	3·84	3·84

another important test of significance equivalent to an F test and this should be studied in a statistical text book. It is especially important in genetics and other fields where observed and expected frequencies are compared.

Analysis of variance. This method for testing the significance of the effect of treatment by the F test (Table 5C) may be considered first in a rather theoretical manner adapted from FISHER (1963). Suppose that each value of the variate (fresh weight) is made up of two parts, T due to treatment and R due to all other (random or uncontrolled) causes, and that these have independent normal distributions with variances σ_T^2 and σ_R^2 respectively. Then the whole variate (T+R) will also be normally distributed, with variance $(\sigma_T^2 + \sigma_R^2)$. If we could take a sample of N_T values of the T part ($N_T = 2$ treatments in the present example) and to each of these add a different sample of N_R values of the R part ($N_R = 8$ replicates) we should have N_T families or arrays each of N_R values of the whole variate. The T part would be the same for all the members of an array, but might well differ from one array to another. From such a set of $N_T N_R$ values we could estimate variances contributed by treatment and by uncontrolled causes. The latter could be directly estimated as the *variance within arrays*

$$s_R^2 = \frac{\sum\sum (x - \bar{x}_T)^2}{N_T(N_R - 1)}$$

where the deviations of the individual observations x from their own array mean $\bar{x}_T$ are squared, summed and then summed again over the various arrays. The mean $\bar{x}_T$ for any array is made up of a T part with variance σ_T^2 and an R part which is the mean of N_R values of R and has therefore a variance σ_R^2/N_R. The variance of the array means about the general mean $\bar{x}$ is therefore estimated as

$$s_T^2 + \frac{s_R^2}{N_R} = \frac{\sum (\bar{x}_T - \bar{x})^2}{N_T - 1}$$

However, this variance is in terms of a mean $(\bar{x}_T)$ of N_R values and to make it comparable with s_R^2 we must multiply it by N_R:

$$N_R s_T^2 + s_R^2 = \frac{N_R \cdot \sum (\bar{x}_T - \bar{x})^2}{N_T - 1}$$

This is our estimate of the *variance between arrays* as used in the so called analysis of variance; it contains both s_T^2 and s_R^2 so that it estimates the variance of the total quantity T+R. It is not, however, equal to the total variance of all the values x about the general mean, $\sum (x - \bar{x})^2/(N_T N_R - 1)$, because the N_R values in each array have a common T part and are not, therefore, independent.

If we were really to analyze the variance into the portions contributed by the two causes we should estimate the variance within arrays s_R^2, and also the variance due to arrays (treatments) as

$$N_R s_T^2 = \frac{N_R \cdot \sum (\bar{x}_T - \bar{x})^2}{N_T - 1} - s_R^2$$

Actually we analyze the total degrees of freedom and the total sum of squares.

Thus $N_T N_R - 1 = N_T(N_R - 1) + (N_T - 1)$

                  Total   Within arrays   Between arrays

and $\sum (x - \bar{x})^2 = \sum\sum (x - \bar{x}_T)^2 + N_R \sum (\bar{x}_T - \bar{x})^2$

              Total   Within arrays   Between arrays

In the simplest case, with only two arrays, samples or treatments, as in Table 5, the analysis of variance method with the F test is exactly equivalent to the method using the *t* test and should give the same estimate of probability (Table 5, *A* and *C*). By either method we test the zero hypothesis that the two samples belong to the same population i.e. that they are really homogeneous, but we now ask the question: 'does the variance estimated between treatment means,

$$\frac{N_R\{(\bar{x}_{GA} - \bar{x})^2 + (\bar{x}_{(1)} - \bar{x})^2\}}{(N_T - 1)}$$

where $N_R = N_{GA} = N_{(1)}$, bear such a high ratio F to that calculated independently and in the same units within treatments,

$$\frac{\sum (x_{GA} - \bar{x}_{GA})^2 + \sum (x_{(1)} - \bar{x}_{(1)})^2}{(N_{GA} - 1) + (N_{(1)} - 1)} \qquad (cf. \textbf{2.2} \text{ p.43})$$

that we should be unwilling to attribute this F value to random variation in a single population?' Or in general terms, does the variance between arrays $(N_R s_T^2 + s_R^2)$ significantly exceed the variance within arrays s_R^2? On the zero hypothesis these are two independent estimates of the same random variance σ_R^2; there is no difference in the effects of the treatments so $N_R \sigma_T^2$ is zero and the true (population) value of F is unity.

If the zero hypothesis is incorrect the between treatment variance will include, in addition to the random component σ_R^2, a component due to treatment $N_R \sigma_T^2$; this must increase it, for variances being based on deviations squared are always positive. The between treatment variance may therefore be equal to or exceed the within treatment variance—it cannot 'really' be less. That is why F is tabulated as a one-tailed test. If the within treatment variance is found greater than that between treatments this result is attributed to chance, and if such an F value is apparently very 'significant' the experiment is suspect and should be examined critically.

In the method just discussed N_R must be the same in each array, but only slight modification is needed to adapt it to different numbers in the arrays (see text books of statistics).

The process of analysis of variance is not restricted to two treatments, as is the *t* test. Where several treatments are included F tests the *average* effect of treatment; in other words, do the treatment means belong to a homogeneous population, as in a uniformity trial with dummy treatments, or is the variation among them greater than would be expected from random sampling of such a population? More elaborate examples of analysis of variance will be given in Chapter 3.

Design of Experiments 3

3.1 Replication and randomization

The last chapter should have made it clear that each treatment in an experiment must be applied to a number of individuals from a population if misleading results are to be improbable. Even so, it is not enough to record for each treatment the total or mean value only of the variate. In such a unique comparison of the results of two experimental treatments the observed difference is made up in unknown proportions of effects, if any, of the treatments themselves and of all the chance differences in other factors which may affect the variate; we cannot estimate the confidence to be placed on the apparent treatment effect found, which is therefore almost useless. This leads to the principle of *replication*: that all experimental comparisons must be repeated, either in space or in time or both. In true replication each individual treatment, which may be a combination treatment in a factorial experiment (p. 10), is applied to two or more *replicates* (single individuals or groups of individuals from the same population) for which the data are recorded separately. The variation within treatments among the replicates must provide an unbiased estimate of the random or uncontrolled part of the variation between those individuals or groups given different treatments which are to be compared; this makes it possible to obtain valid estimates of significance and confidence limits for the treatment effects.

The danger of so called 'look-see trials' with only a single sample for each treatment, no matter how large the number of individuals involved, may be further illustrated from another uniformity trial. Fig. 3–1 shows the

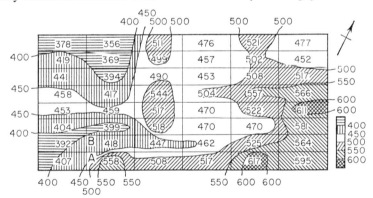

Fig. 3–1 Yields of cabbages, harvested 14.7.58–13.8.58, in lbs per 0·011 acre plot ($\equiv$ kg per 0·0098 hectare) from a uniformity trial. Yield contours sketched on assumption that mean yield for each plot occurred in the centre.

yields of cabbages from 48 similarly treated plots in an apparently uniform and level field and each value represents the total weights of some 350 plants. Suppose that only the two plots marked A and B had been planted with cabbages, to test a new commercial fertilizer mixture. If by chance plot A was chosen for the fertilizer treatment with B used as a 'control', and if the fertilizer was in fact entirely without effect, we should conclude that it had increased yield by 33 per cent; conversely, if the fertilizer was applied to B it would have to increase yield by at least 33 per cent or we should regard it as actively harmful. Even if we weighed and recorded each cabbage separately in such a trial, the individual cabbages on each plot would not be replicates of the respective treatments. Their weights would vary because of differences in genetic constitution, spacing, competition from weeds, local soil differences within the plot and innumerable other factors; the uncontrolled variation between cabbages given the two different treatments would be due to all such sources but also to the major differences in initial soil fertility between the two plots. For valid replicates we must use other plots, preferably of similar size and shape, given the same treatments.

It is also possible to have replication in time instead of, or as well as, in space with a given plot or plots having each of the treatments for N_R seasons in a completely random order. This would be particularly unsuitable for fertilizer experiments because of residual effects of treatments persisting from one season to the next (p. 13).

The simplest type of design for a field experiment has the N_T treatments allotted strictly at random (p. 10) among the available plots, preferably so that there is an equal number (N_R) of plots of each treatment. This is unquestionably valid (i.e. fair), for every one of the possible sets of N_R plots has an equal chance of having the same treatment and so being used to estimate random variation; the criterion of true replication is therefore satisfied and over a large number of similar experiments, each randomized afresh, the mean treatment effects will be accurately estimated. Unless N_R is very large, however, individual experiments may yield results which vary considerably from the mean, although the test of their significance will be valid; in other words the accuracy of individual experiments will be low but we shall generally be aware that it is. For example, if 8 fertilizer treatments were applied at random to the 48 plots shown in Fig. 3–1, so that there were 6 plots of each, it might happen by chance that nearly all the plots of one particular treatment were grouped together in the E corner; the high basic fertility of these plots would then make that treatment appear unduly good, though perhaps not significantly so. When such a grouping occurs during randomization there is a temptation to reject it and try again but this must be resisted or the test of significance will be vitiated.

In the past a great many field experiments were carried out with *systematic designs* intended to spread the treatments uniformly over the area used. For example, a favourite type of design, with say four treatments, was as follows:

A B C D A B
C D A B C D
A B C D A B   etc.

Such designs make a valid test of significance impossible and an element of randomization is an essential part of replication. Variation in soil fertility has been shown by numerous uniformity trials to be systematic rather than random: in general the fertility of adjacent plots is more alike than that of widely separated ones. If, therefore, a systematic arrangement has plots with different treatments closely adjacent (as above) a very precise comparison of the treatments will be obtained. Unfortunately, the closeness of the differently treated plots results in the replicates of the same treatments being widely separated and it is on these that the estimate of random variation is based. This is therefore a gross overestimate of the uncontrolled part of the variation between treatments and our comparison, although made more precise by the design, will appear in the test of significance to be less so. Conversely, if we arrange for the replicates to be closely adjacent and the differently treated plots are therefore separated widely, the comparison of the treatments will be made less precise but owing to the closeness of the replicates will appear to be more so. The way out of this dilemma is to allot the treatments at random so that there are N_R plots of each; on the average the differences in basic fertility between replicate plots will then be similar to those between plots having the various possible pairs of treatments and the random variation within treatments will give a valid estimate of the uncontrolled portion of the variation between treatments.

3.2 Restrictions on random arrangement

We have seen that although a completely randomized design of experiment is valid it may sometimes be extremely inaccurate; we are unlikely to be misled but we may fail to disprove the zero hypothesis and demonstrate effects of the applied treatments. It is often possible, by partial restriction of the randomization, to remove from the treatment comparisons the effects of some of the larger sources of uncontrolled variation (which thus become 'controlled' like additional treatments)—these *must* then also be removed from the estimate of random variation used in testing the significance of treatment effects.

3.2.1 *The paired sample method*

This has already been briefly discussed (p. 14) and is the simplest type of design with a restriction on randomization. In the radish experiment discussed on p. 44 we might have numbered the plots of 4 experimental plants in ascending order of their total leaf areas, either estimated by eye or measured, and then allotted the GA and (1) treatments at random in each successive pair of plots. The plots in these pairs would be as alike as possible in leaf area and since the values of the variate used to assess treatment effect (fresh weight) would depend to a large extent on initial leaf area, both because of the weight of the leaves and their photosynthetic production, the uncontrolled variation between the two treatments (within pairs) would be much reduced. The relatively large variation in fresh weight between pair means having been eliminated from the treatment comparison, it would also have to be removed from the estimate of so called 'error' used to test the significance of the treatment effect. This could be done by using the series of differences $GA - (1)$, calculated within each pair, as data for the calculation of s^2. Both the mean treatment effect and its estimated standard error ($\sqrt{s^2/N_P}$, where N_P was the number of pairs) would then be unaffected by the variation between the pair means. However, as suggested earlier (p. 14), if the pairs covered a very wide range the individual treatment responses might be appreciably affected, for example, plants with larger leaf area might respond more to GA. This would represent an *interaction* (p. 12) between leaf area and GA, which indicates that such pairs are not in fact true replicates but represent levels of an additional factor (leaf area) in a factorial design. The variation in the series of differences, estimated by s^2, is a measure of random variation plus this interaction. If the mean difference is found significantly different from zero, this indicates that the treatment effect is sufficiently consistent throughout the leaf area range used to outweigh the interaction (if any) and it may therefore be expected to apply approximately to plants of various sizes. The wider the range over which a significant treatment effect is found, the more general is the application of the finding. Such use of an interaction as the basis of 'error' for testing the significance of an average treatment effect is further discussed later. There are no true replicates in the present example but the $GA - (1)$ comparison is repeated in the different leaf area classes and this is sometimes called 'hidden replication'. If inspection of the data in such an experiment suggests a large and consistent interaction, possibly resulting in a non-significant mean treatment effect, it may be valuable to carry out another factorial experiment with true replicates to assess the type and significance of the interaction. This would involve at least two plots of each treatment in each leaf area class, allotted randomly.

t test. Leaf area data are not available for the radish plants but a similar exercise may be carried out with some of the data shown in Fig. 3-1. In Table 8A the yields for the 16 plots at the north-east end of the field have been grouped into 8 pairs, on the *a priori* assumption that adjacent plots are probably more alike in basic fertility than more distant ones, and two fictitious treatments (fertilizer or no fertilizer, denoted by f and (1)) have been allotted at random within the pairs. The series of 8 differences $(x_{f-(1)})$ has been used as data; the mean treatment effect found ($+2 \cdot 9$ lbs) is much smaller than its estimated standard error ($18 \cdot 3$ lbs) and therefore

Table 8 Experiment with paired samples. Yields of cabbage in lbs per 0·011 acre plot (=kg per 0·0098 hectare) from 16 plots at north-east end of uniformity trial shown in Fig. 3–1, allotted two fictitious fertilizer treatments in paired plots.

A   Significance of mean treatment effect by *t* test

x_f	$x_{(1)}$	$x_{f-(1)}$	$\sum x_P$
521	502	+19	1023
508	557	−49	1065
470	522	−52	992
617	525	+92	1142
477	452	+25	929
566	517	+49	1083
581	611	−30	1192
564	595	−31	1159

$$\sum x_f = 4304 \qquad \sum x_{(1)} = 4281 \qquad \sum x_{f-(1)} = +23 \qquad \sum\sum x_P = 8585$$
$$\bar{x}_f = 538\cdot000 \qquad \bar{x}_{(1)} = 535\cdot125 \qquad \bar{x}_{f-(1)} = +2\cdot875 \qquad \bar{x}_P = 536\cdot5625$$

$$s^2 = \sum (x_{f-(1)} - \bar{x}_{f-(1)})^2/(N_P - 1)$$
$$= \{\sum x_{f-(1)}^2 - (\sum x_{f-(1)})^2/N_P\} \div (N_P - 1) = 2678\cdot70$$
$$\mathrm{E}_{\bar{x}_{f-(1)}} = \sqrt{s^2/N_P} \qquad\qquad = 18\cdot30 \text{ lbs}$$
$$t = (\bar{x}_{f-(1)} - 0)/\mathrm{E}_{\bar{x}_{f-(1)}} \qquad = 0\cdot157$$
$$n = 7$$
$$P = 0\cdot8$$

Confidence limits of $\bar{x}_{f-(1)}$ for P0·05 $= \bar{x}_{f-(1)} \pm t_{.05}\mathrm{E}_{\bar{x}_{f-(1)}} = +2\cdot875 \pm 2\cdot36 \times 18\cdot30$
(where $t_{.05}$ is the value of *t* for P0·05 and $n = 7$) $= +46\cdot2$ and $-40\cdot4$ lbs

---

B   Analysis of variance (in terms of 1 plot yield)

Sums of squares, using an assumed mean of 0

Total	$\sum (x - \bar{x})^2 = \sum x^2 - (\sum x)^2/N$	$= 4643937 - 4606389\cdot1$
		$= 37547\cdot9$
Treatment	$N_P \sum (\bar{x}_T - \bar{x})^2 = [\sum (\sum x_T)^2/N_P] - (\sum x)^2/N$	$= 4606422\cdot1 - 4606389\cdot1$
		$= 33\cdot0$
Pairs	$N_T \sum (\bar{x}_P - \bar{x})^2 = [\sum (\sum x_P)^2/N_T] - (\sum x)^2/N$	$= 4634528\cdot5 - 4606389\cdot1$
		$= 28139\cdot4$

Variation	Degrees of freedom	Sum of squares	Variance	F
Total	$N-1 = 15$	$37547\cdot9$	—	—
Between pairs P	$N_P - 1 = 7$	$28139\cdot4$	$s_P^2 = 4019\cdot9$	$s_P^2/s_{TP}^2 = 3\cdot00$
Between treatments T (within pairs)	$N_T - 1 = 1$	$33\cdot0$	$s_T^2 = 33\cdot0$	$s_T^2/s_{TP}^2 < 1$ ($0\cdot0246 = t^2$)
Residue (TP interaction)	$(N_T-1)(N_P-1) = 7$	$9375\cdot5$	$s_{TP}^2 = 1339.4$	—
Or, ignoring 'treatments',				
Between pairs P	$N_P - 1 = 7$	$28139\cdot4$	$s_P^2 = 4019\cdot9$	$s_P^2/s_W^2 = 3\cdot42$
Within pairs W	$N_P(N_T-1) = 8$	$9408\cdot5$	$s_W^2 = 1176\cdot1$	

(F required for P0·05 = 3·50, so pair effect almost significant)

---

entirely non-significant. With 8 values ($N_P=8$) there are 7 degrees of freedom for estimating s^2, whereas had the random arrangement not been restricted there would have been 14 as in Table 5*A*. For the paired sample method to improve precision, therefore, the two values of the variate in each pair must not only be positively correlated (that is, tend to rise or fall together, giving more uniform differences) but sufficiently so to outweigh the loss of half the degrees of freedom with the consequent increase in the value of t needed for significance (p. 43). The choice of the basis for pairing therefore calls for a great deal of judgement and a purely random arrangement may be better.

Analysis of variance. The paired sample data may also be analysed by the method of analysis of variance (p. 48) and the F test, which is here exactly equivalent to the use of differences and the t test. The analysis is shown in Table 8*B* and discussed below, being identical with that for the randomized block method, with pairs corresponding to blocks; the residue or 'error' variance is that for treatment × pairs interaction. In Table 8*B* this variance is 1339·4, whereas in Table 8*A* s^2 is 2678·7. This is because the analysis of variance has been carried out in terms of a single plot yield, while the analysis for the t test is in terms of differences between two plot yields. The variance of a difference (or sum) of two independent quantities is the sum of their variances (p. 34). In the lower part of Table 8*B* the degree of freedom for the two fictitious 'treatments' and the corresponding fortuitously small sum of squares have been added to the residue, which becomes 'within pairs'. The F value for pairs is now very nearly significant at P0·05, showing (probably) a real reduction in variability due to the removal of pair to pair differences.

3.2.2   The randomized block method

The use of paired samples is a special case of the randomized block method, in which the experimental plants, animals, plots or other units are arranged in groups or 'blocks', each as uniform as can be conveniently achieved in respect of some attribute considered important; there are usually as many units in a block as there are treatments, and the latter are allotted at random with the restriction that each treatment occurs once in each block. There may, however, be two or more units for each treatment within each block, also randomized; these may be used for successive samples during the experiment, or as true replicates to test the significance of the interaction of treatments and blocks (p. 53). There is no absolute limit to the total number of units per block, but the larger the blocks the less uniform they will be and therefore the smaller the gain in precision over a completely random arrangement.

The randomized block layout is undoubtedly the most generally useful and flexible experimental design. It provides a much better alternative to picking out a single limited class of relatively uniform material for experimentation (p. 28): a random sample can be taken from the whole available population and graded into relatively uniform blocks in respect of a suitable attribute, as indicated for pairs in the previous section. The experimental results will then apply to the population as a whole. If the attribute used is not thought to be of particular interest except to improve precision, the blocks of this attribute may coincide with blocks of position thus further increasing precision; information on the effect of the attribute will then be inseparable from (*confounded* with) positional effects. If one or more units in a randomized block experiment are lost through accident it is possible to discard a whole block, or even to discard one or more treatments throughout the experiment if they are not part of a factorial design.

Some possible examples of randomized block experiments are: nutritional experiments with young mice or piglets, using litters as blocks and thus eliminating parentage from treatment comparisons; experiments on germination or seedling growth using a random sample of seed graded into seed weight classes as blocks (the problems of taking a random sample of seed merit thought—p. 28); experiments on effects of synthetic plant hormones in delaying senescence of leaf discs—if as many discs can be cut from a single leaf as there are treatments, leaf to leaf differences can be eliminated as blocks.

In plot experiments in field or garden, or in glasshouse experiments, the blocks should normally be as compact (and therefore as square) as possible, but do not have to be all of the same shape nor contiguous; if however there is prior knowledge of a gradient in some important factor, such as light or temperature in a glasshouse or fertility or soil depth due to a slope (p. 29) in the field, it may be an advantage to elongate the blocks across the gradient and so make each block more uniform; plots should then be elongated along the gradient.

Randomized blocks of time can be very useful if we have a complicated apparatus in which we can only experiment with one plant, leaf, animal or other unit at a time. The various treatments are carried out in a random order and each one with a different unit, possibly at the same time on successive days but otherwise keeping each block of time as compact as possible; the blocks can come at long intervals. When all the treatments have been completed once, a new and freshly randomized block is carried out and so on. Any seasonal effects on the material, between blocks, are then eliminated. Alternatively, we may use a single unit throughout each block (p. 13); treatment comparisons are then within units instead of between units and should be more precise if the unit does not deteriorate or improve; unit to unit differences are confounded with blocks of time. It is essential either to use a new unit for each treatment, so that treatment comparisons and the estimate of residual variation are both entirely between units, or to use a single unit throughout the block so that both are within units; the only exception to this rule is if some form of 'split plot' design is used (see below p. 63).

Analysis of variance. As an example, the final dry weights of radish plants in a water culture experiment carried out in class are analyzed in Table 9.

The four blocks represent pairs of students and also positions in the glass-house; the treatments form a $2 \times 2 \times 2$ factorial experiment, with $\frac{1}{50}$ or full supply of nitrogen, phosphorus and potassium in all the 8 possible combinations, but for the purposes of preliminary analysis (Table 9A)

Table 9 2^3 factorial experiment in 4 randomized blocks. Log$_{10}$ dry weight (mg) per 2 radish plants sampled 27.5.46 after 33 days growth in water culture. Eight treatments, with nitrogen, phosphorus and potassium at full (N, P or K) or $\frac{1}{50}$ supply (no symbol); all three at $\frac{1}{50}$ level shown by ( ).

A Preliminary analysis of variance (pp. 56–62)

Block	( )	N	P	NP	K	NK	KP	NPK	$\sum x_B$
				Log$_{10}$ dry weight (mg)					
I	1·67	1·90	1·74	2·23	2·00	2·13	1·89	2·43	15·99
II	1·53	1·69	1·53	1·85	1·94	2·07	2·07	2·73	15·41
III	1·92	1·92	1·77	1·81	2·05	2·00	1·96	2·63	16·06
IV	1·46	1·77	1·60	2·06	1·77	2·04	1·93	2·49	15·12
$\sum x_T$	6·58	7·28	6·64	7·95	7·76	8·24	7·85	10·28	62·58
$\bar{x}_T$	1·6450	1·8200	1·6600	1·9875	1·9400	2·0600	1·9625	2·5700	1·955625

Sums of squares, using assumed mean o

Total, $\qquad \sum (x - \bar{x})^2 = \sum x^2 - (\sum x)^2 / N \quad = 125\cdot1904 - 122\cdot3830$
$$= 2\cdot8074$$

Treatment, $N_B \sum (\bar{x}_T - \bar{x})^2 = \{\sum (\sum x_T)^2 / N_B\} - (\sum x)^2 / N = 124.7508 - 122.3830$
$$= 2\cdot3678$$

Block, $\qquad N_T \sum (\bar{x}_B - \bar{x})^2 = \{\sum (\sum x_B)^2 / N_T\} - (\sum x)^2 / N = 122\cdot4608 - 122\cdot3830$
$$= 0\cdot0778$$

Variation	Degrees of freedom		Sum of squares	Variance	F	F for	
						P0·20	P0·001
Total	$N-1$	$= 31$	2·8074	—			
Treatment T	$N_T - 1$	$= 7$	2·3678	0·33826	19·6		5·6
Block B	$N_B - 1$	$= 3$	0·0778	0·02593	1·5	1·6	
Residue TB	$(N_T - 1)(N_B - 1)$	$= 21$	0·3622	0·01725			

(Treatment effect highly significant; block effect non-significant)

Confidence limits for a treatment mean $= \bar{x}_T \pm t_{.05} \sqrt{s_{TB}^2 / N_B}$
$$= \bar{x}_T \pm 2\cdot08 \sqrt{0\cdot01725/4}$$
$$= \bar{x}_T \pm 0\cdot1366$$

Least significant difference (P0·05) $= 2\cdot08 \sqrt{2 \times 0\cdot01725/4} = 0\cdot1932$

( )	P	N	K	KP	NP	NK	NPK
1·645	1·660	1·820	1·940	1·963	1·988	2·060	2·570

Bracketed means do not differ significantly.
De-transformed (anti-log) treatment means (mg)

( )	P	N	K	KP	NP	NK	NPK
44·2	45·7	66·1	87·1	91·8	97·3	114·8	371·5

Bracketed means do not differ significantly

B   Further analysis of treatment effect (pp. 66–67)

Three 2-way tables needed e.g.

Means of high and low K

	$\frac{1}{50}$N	Full N	Mean
$\frac{1}{50}$P	1·79250	1·94000	1.86625
Full P	1·81125	2·27875	2·04500
Mean	1·80188	2·10937	1·955625

Mean effect of N $= 2\cdot10937 - 1\cdot80188$	$=$	$+0\cdot30749$
Sum of squares for N $= 0\cdot30749^2 \times 32/4$	$=$	$0\cdot75645$
Mean effect of P $= 2\cdot04500 - 1\cdot86625$	$=$	$+0\cdot17875$
Sum of squares for P $= 0\cdot17875^2 \times 32/4$	$=$	$0\cdot25561$
Interaction NP $= \{(2\cdot27875 + 1\cdot79250) - (1\cdot94000 + 1\cdot81125)\}/2 =$		$+0\cdot16000$
Sum of squares for NP $= 0\cdot16000^2 \times 32/4$	$=$	$0\cdot20480$

	Effects	*t*	P
N	+0·30749	6·62	<0·001
P	+0·17875	3·85	0·001
NP	+0·16000	3·45	<0·01
K	+0·35500	7·65	<0·001
NK	+0·05625	1·21	<0·3
KP	+0·08750	1·88	<0·1
NPK	+0·08375	1·80	<0·1

Standard error for difference of 2 means of 16 $= \sqrt{2 \times 0\cdot01725/16} = 0\cdot04643$;
(for use with above 'effects') $n = 21$

Variation	Degrees of freedom	Variance	F
N	1	0·75645	43·9 (P<0·001)
P	1	0·25561	14·8 (P 0·001)
NP	1	0·20480	11·9 (P<0·01)
K	1	1·00820	58·4 (P<0·001)
NK	1	0·02531	1·5 (P<0·3)
KP	1	0·06125	3·6 (P<0·1)
NPK	1	0·05611	3·3 (P<0·1)
TB	21	0·01725	

Standard error for difference of 2 means of 8 $= \sqrt{2 \times 0\cdot01725/8} = 0\cdot06564$;
(for use within NP 2-way table) $n = 21$

we will consider them simply as 8 independent treatments. The data have been transformed (p. 34) to logarithms for reasons which will be discussed later. We now need to split up the total degrees of freedom and the corresponding sum of squares into three parts, for the variate is considered to be made up not of two (p. 48) but of three components: one due to treatments, one to blocks and one to uncontrolled causes. In terms of deviations from the true mean μ we postulate that for any unit, with say treatment i in block j, the yield is

$$y_{ij} = \mu + \tau_i + \beta_j + R_{ij}$$

where τ and β are the deviations due to the true treatment and block effects respectively and R is the residual deviation. We make a series of separate zero hypotheses: that τ is zero; that β is zero, and also that if they are not zero then their effects are independent and additive so that R is purely random with no component $(\tau\beta)$ due to interaction.

The use of the interaction term as 'error'. We can see from the two-way table of log weights in Table 9A that a randomized block experiment with each treatment represented once in each block is in fact an unreplicated factorial experiment (p. 10), for each block is different just as is each treatment. The values in the body of the table are subject to variation due to average treatment effects, to average block effects, to interaction (if any) of treatments and blocks, that is to the treatment effects being different in different blocks and *vice versa*, and finally, as with all experimental data, to random causes. From the total sum of squares $\sum (x - \bar{x})^2$, calculated within the two-way table, we subtract the average treatment sum of squares $N_B\sum (\bar{x}_T - \bar{x})^2$ and the average block sum of squares $N_T\sum (\bar{x}_B - \bar{x})^2$; these are here shown as calculated from the marginal means—note that they are multiplied by the number of units making up each mean and are therefore in terms of a single unit (p. 48). Similarly, in the calculations made with an assumed mean of zero in Table 9A, e.g. $\dfrac{\sum (\sum x_T)^2}{N_B} - \dfrac{(\sum x)^2}{N}$ for the treatment sum of squares, the marginal totals have been used and the crude sum of squares is therefore divided by the number of units making up each total. The residual sum of squares, when divided by the corresponding degrees of freedom, gives an estimate of random variance plus the component if any due to interaction; the latter could only be detected by comparison with a random variance calculated from true replicates of the treatments within the blocks. Even if there were such replicates, the interaction variance would be preferable for testing the significance of treatment, for effects found significant against interaction with blocks are large and consistent enough to override the positional interaction and therefore more likely to apply elsewhere.

The interaction of treatment and time almost always provides the best basis for 'error' in biological experiments; all biological material changes with time, and treatment effects found significant against this interaction are more likely to be repeatable (p. 20). Experiments should therefore be carried out in randomized blocks of time (p. 56) or better still in several randomized blocks separated in space and repeated on several occasions independently, i.e. in freshly randomized positions. We can then test treatment effects both ways.

5

t tests. If the average effect of treatment is found significant by the F test (p. 49) it is usual to test the significance of the difference between pairs of individual treatment means by the *t* test, using the treatment and block interaction variance (s_{TB}^2) as 'error' i.e.

$$t = \{(\bar{x}_1 - \bar{x}_2) - 0\}/\sqrt{2s_{TB}^2/N_B}$$

Alternatively, a 'least significant difference' is calculated for say P0·05 as: L.S.D. $= t_{.05}\sqrt{2s_{TB}^2/N_B}$, where $t_{.05}$ is the value of *t* for the appropriate number of degrees of freedom n and P0·05. This is then used to group those treatment means which do not differ significantly, in a list arranged in order of magnitude (Table 9*A*). This procedure is liable to suggest erroneously 'significant' results when many means are included, though some safeguard is provided by the F test. If the latter does not show a significant treatment effect, the treatment means may well belong to a single homogeneous population; with 8 treatments there are $(8 \times 7)/2 = 28$ possible pairs, so that we might expect at least one pair to be apparently significant at $P < 0·05$ (1 in 20) and for comparing the largest and smallest we should use a value of P in the *t* table of $1/(20 \times 28) = 0·002$. If we find a significant F for treatment it is unlikely that we are dealing with a uniformity trial and these odds do not apply. However, it is still likely that the largest and smallest means will have positive and negative deviations respectively from their 'true' values, so that the value of P will be underestimated if they are selected for test *because* they are the extremes. The comparisons to be made should always be decided upon before inspection of the results; otherwise we shall tend to select out the largest differences which are those most likely to be overestimated. Such problems are discussed further in COCHRAN and COX (1957, sections 3·53 and 3·54a). Ideally, significant effects of interest but which the experiment was not planned to test should be deliberately investigated in further experiments.

Even if the average effect of treatment is not significant it is always legitimate to abstract from each block the data for a pair of treatments or groups of treatments of particular interest and use the *t* test as in Table 8*A*. This has the advantage of isolating the components of the residual variance provided by the treatments being compared but the degrees of freedom for 'error' are reduced to $(N_B - 1)$.

Transformations. The use of a single estimate of residual (or 'error') variance in an analysis of variance assumes that the residual deviations R (p. 59) for all the units are normally distributed with the same 'true' variance σ^2. The most important implication of this is that the residual variances within the different treatments, although subject to random variation, should be independent of the magnitude of the treatment means. The first objective of all transformations is to achieve this and the second, to make the distribution more nearly normal. When treatment effects are very large, as with age effects on size of rapidly growing plants or nutrient effects in sand or water culture, the treatments having the larger means generally have larger variances. For the raw dry weight data for the example in Table 9A, estimates $\sum (x-\bar{x}_{\mathrm{T}})^2/3$ (which included variation due to differences between blocks in each case) were compared in pairs by the F test (p. 46); that for NPK was much the largest and significantly greater than all others except NP. The logarithmic transformation made the variances much more homogeneous and apparently independent of the magnitude of the means. This transformation is appropriate when the variance for the raw data is approximately proportional to the (mean)^2.

Data in the form of small whole numbers often tend to be distributed in a Poisson distribution. Examples are the numbers of bacterial colonies in Petri dish cultures, or of weeds or insects of a given species in quadrats or small plots; necessary conditions are that each individual occurs within an area at random and independently of other individuals (i.e. without mutual attraction or repulsion), and that the individuals are numerous enough for many of the areas counted to be occupied by one or more. In this distribution the variance is equal to the mean and therefore proportional to it. The appropriate transformation is to use square roots of the original data for analysis, if the numbers (x) for each area are between 10 and 100, or $\sqrt{x+\frac{1}{2}}$ if x is generally less than 10. If most of the numbers are over 100 a transformation is unlikely to be needed.

Fractions or percentages (based on whole numbers), representing the proportion of individuals out of a fixed total belonging to a particular category, tend to be distributed in a binomial distribution and then the variance is maximal at 50 per cent, decreasing symmetrically to zero at 0 per cent and 100 per cent. An example would be the percentages of plants flowering as a result of photoperiodic treatments in a glasshouse experiment. For such data the angular (or inverse sine) transformation is appropriate. Analysis is carried out on the angles, between 0° and 90°, whose sines equal the square roots of the fractions. These have been tabulated by FISHER and YATES (1963). If percentages (p) lie between 30 and 70, however, the variance is nearly independent of the mean and no transformation is needed; if they are all below 20, the variance is almost proportional to the mean and a square root transformation may be used, as also on $(100-p)$ if they are all above 80.

For further discussion of transformations see COCHRAN (1938) and BARTLETT (1947).

The use of transformed data alters the meaning of absence of interaction, which for the raw data has been defined as the treatment effects being independent and additive (p. 12). With a log transformation, lack of interaction implies that the treatment effects on log yields are independent and additive; for the raw data, therefore, a multiplicative interaction holds, that is, a given increase in the level of one factor (or treatment) multiplies the yield by a constant whatever the levels of the other factors. In some systems this may be thought to be a more appropriate definition of independence of the factors than that their effects are additive for the raw data; for example, the effects of factors on numbers of bacteria may be expected to be proportional to the numbers of cells present and therefore additive on a log scale. In practice, however, it does not make a great difference which of the two definitions is accepted unless the responses to two factors concerned are both proportionally large.

I have yet to see a satisfying interpretation of the biological implications of lack of interaction in terms of angles!

3.2.3   Latin squares

In these a further restriction is placed upon the random arrangement of treatments among the experimental units. If there are N treatments there have to be N units of each. In a field experiment the plots are normally arranged in the form of a square of N rows and N columns; each of the N treatments occurs once in each row and once in each column but subject to this restriction the arrangement is randomized (see FISHER and YATES, 1963). An example of a 5×5 latin square is given below

$$
\begin{array}{ccccc}
B & A & D & C & E \\
A & C & E & D & B \\
D & B & C & E & A \\
E & D & A & B & C \\
C & E & B & A & D \\
\end{array}
$$

There are $N^2 - 1 = 24$ degrees of freedom, of which $N - 1 = 4$ represent treatment effect, 4 row effect, 4 column effect and the residual 12 provide an estimate of 'error' for testing these effects. Interactions cannot be tested as these are confounded—thus the differences in effects of the treatments in the various rows (treatment × row interaction) will be partly due to their positions in columns. Each of these two-factor interactions would involve $4 \times 4 = 16$ degrees of freedom so that there are obviously not enough degrees of freedom to disentangle them.

The sums of squares are calculated much as in Table 9A. The residual variance provides a valid estimate of 'error' if the arrangement has been properly randomized, for every pair of plots not in the same row or the same column will have an equal chance of belonging to the same treatment.

This arrangement is completely balanced about the centre of the square and eliminates effects of fertility gradients in two directions at right angles, both from the estimate of 'error' and from treatment comparisons; the latter can therefore be of much increased precision where gradients occur. The arrangement of the plots need not be in a square; for example the rows could be placed end to end:

B A D C E;   A C E D B;   D B C E A;   E D A B C;   C E B A D.

Variation between rows and average fertility gradient within rows would then be eliminated.

The latin square becomes unwieldy with a large number of treatments;

with only three treatments it is unsatisfactory because there are only two degrees of freedom for 'error' and because there is too small a population of possible 3 × 3 squares from which to make a random choice—the same arrangements therefore recur too often. Another disadvantage is that if one or more plots are accidentally spoiled the experiment is no longer balanced. It is also frequently found that variations in soil fertility occur in irregular patches rather than regular gradients (Fig. 3–1) and then a randomized block design is likely to give greater precision.

Latin squares may be valuable in serial experiments where only a few experimental units are available. Thus effects of five diets on live weight gain could be tested with only five piglets, rows representing periods of time (preferably separated by a 'settling down' period for each new diet) and columns the individual piglets. Average differences due to age and between piglets would thus be eliminated. Even with settling down periods the hazard of after-effects of some diets upon the responses to others would remain.

Latin squares may be used to eliminate between-plant variation and also 'leaf age' differences within plants, where treatment effects are known or can be assumed not to spread from one leaf to another, e.g. with detached leaves or leaf discs. A 4 × 4 latin square could be used to investigate effects on leaf senescence of two synthetic growth substances each applied at 0 and 1 dose factorially combined. Four plants would be represented by columns in the analysis and four leaf positions by rows. Colorimetric estimations of chlorophyll content could be used as the measure of senescence. It should be remembered, in interpreting the results, that leaves at different positions on the plant often have other systematic differences besides those due to age (RICHARDS, 1934). It might perhaps be found that plant effect (columns) was quite non-significant and that a better discrimination of treatment effects would have been obtained with 4 randomized blocks of leaf position, giving 9 degrees of freedom for 'error' instead of 6; nevertheless, if the experiment was carried out as a latin square it should be so analyzed, for the variation (between plants) eliminated from the treatment comparisons could never be shown to be zero and should therefore also be eliminated from the estimate of 'error'. This general principle applies to any restriction of full randomization, whether by paired samples (p. 52), randomized blocks (p. 55) or any other method. Such restrictions are not advisable, therefore, if degrees of freedom for 'error' are few, unless we have good reason to think that the variation eliminated is likely to be large.

For a more elaborate example of latin squares, used to eliminate time effects from responses of leaf stomata to carbon dioxide, see HEATH and RUSSELL (1954).

3.2.4 Split plot designs

These occur frequently in biological experiments; often they are used unwittingly and are not then properly analyzed. The name derives from factorial field experiments in which certain treatments, such as different depths of ploughing, can only be applied to large plots while for others, such as fertilizers, quite small plots can be used. The layout therefore consists of main plots (ploughing treatments), possibly arranged in randomized blocks, with each main plot subdivided into two or more sub-plots to which the fertilizer treatments are randomly allotted.

The growth substance treatments mentioned in the last section might be combined factorially with 3 levels of nitrogen fertilizer in a split plot design. Perhaps the 3 fertilizer treatments would be applied to 12 potted plants (main units) in 4 randomized blocks in the glasshouse. For each plant the 4 growth substance treatments might be allotted randomly among the 4 youngest fully expanded leaves (sub-units). The degrees of freedom would then be subdivided as follows:

Between main units
   (plants):

Blocks (B)	$(N_B - 1) =$	3
Fertilizer (F)	$(N_F - 1) =$	2
Interaction B × F	$(N_B - 1)(N_F - 1) =$	6
('Error' for B and F)		
Total	$(N_B N_F - 1) =$	11

Within main units
   (Leaves = sub-
   units):

Growth substance (G)	$(N_G - 1) =$	3
G × F	$(N_G - 1)(N_F - 1) =$	6
Residue	$N_F(N_B - 1)(N_G - 1) =$	27
('Error' for G and G × F)		
Total		47

Such a table of degrees of freedom should always be prepared, so as to decide how to analyze any experiment before it is actually carried out. The total sum of squares $\sum (x - \bar{x})^2$ is in terms of one leaf (sub-unit) and the other sums of squares must be multiplied by the numbers of sub-units in the means used, to be comparable (pp. 48 and 59). There are two separate 'error' variances, one for main treatments (F) and the other for the sub-treatments (G) and the interaction (G × F). The sub-treatment error is generally the smaller, because the sub-units are often positively correlated (p. 55), and is also based on more degrees of freedom. Effects of sub-treatments and the interaction are therefore estimated with greater precision than those of the main treatments; hence the latter should preferably be of subsidiary interest. For comparing two main treatment means (F) by the *t* test, a standard error based on the main 'error' variance (B × F) is used; for two sub-treatment means (G) averaged over all main treatments, or for two sub-treatment means within the same main treatment, the standard error is based on the residual variance. However, for comparisons of two main treatments in a single sub-treatment, or in two different sub-treatments, a weighted mean of the two standard errors must be used and the *t* test modified (COCHRAN and COX, 1957).

Variation between and within main units. In glasshouse experiments, different compartments are often maintained at different temperatures, generally unreplicated because of limited facilities, and various treatments are replicated within the compartments; such replicates are often used for testing the significance of the average temperature effect (e.g. HEATH, 1943a, b). These are, of course, split plot experiments and tests of main treatment significance based on replication within compartments are invalid (*cf.* p. 51). Such a test could show, with a stated probability, that the plants in one compartment were 'really' different from those in another, but would give no indication of whether any of this difference was due to the main treatments (temperatures) or whether it was entirely due to positional differences in shading, draughts and other uncontrolled factors. The best method would be to repeat the experiments, with the compartments re-randomized, and use the interaction with time as the basis of 'error' (p. 59). However, with very few compartments many repetitions would be necessary to give a reasonable number of degrees of freedom for 'error'. If the treatments are interchanged frequently between compartments during a single experiment it may be hoped that positional effects will be reduced, though of course they cannot be estimated nor the significance of the main treatments tested.

3.3 Factorial experiments

The classical method of experimentation was to investigate the effects of varying one factor at a time, with all other conditions held as constant as possible. This is of very limited value in biological research, for the responses of an organism to any factor depend markedly on the levels of other factors, so that the responses under a single arbitrarily chosen set of conditions are seldom of much interest. Factorial experiments, in which two or more factors are investigated simultaneously, each at two or more levels and in all possible combinations, enable us to study the type of interaction between the various factors, which is both more interesting and more useful than trying to specify optimum conditions (see chapter on 'Interaction of factors', HEATH, 1969). They are especially valuable in exploratory work; for this purpose the several factors thought to be important should be combined over wide ranges and as many levels as time and facilities will allow. Such large experiments (e.g. HEATH, 1943a, b; HEATH and MATHUR, 1944) provide a general picture from which areas of particular interest can be selected for further investigation. Other merits of wide ranging factorial experiments are that they test hypotheses severely (p. 9), by including treatment combinations that are not specially chosen to support them, and that they often result in new discoveries by subjecting the organism to combinations of conditions not encountered in its evolution

(p. 5); it is important not to omit any combination treatments, even if they look 'silly', both for the above reasons and because this makes proper analysis difficult.

Success with factorial experiments depends on judgement in picking important factors and since an additional factor at only two levels doubles the size of the experiment, for a constant number of replications, we cannot afford many unimportant ones. However, owing to 'hidden replication' (p. 53), large factorial experiments can be carried out with fewer replications than simple experiments, or even with none at all when interactions between four or more factors can be assumed unimportant and used as 'error'.

3.3.1 2^n experiments

Further analysis of treatment effect. The example for a 2^2 factorial (p. 11) shows that all treatment effects are obtained by comparing two halves of the data summed in various ways. In the 2^3 experiment with radishes (Table 9) the individual treatments are:

$$( ), N, P, NP, K, NK, KP \text{ and } NPK,$$

where presence of a symbol indicates high level of that element and absence low level. The average potassium effect is given by the difference between the means of the last four and the first four treatments; the average nitrogen effect is the difference of the means of the even and the odd numbered treatments; that of phosphorus is the mean of the 3rd, 4th, 7th and 8th, less the mean of the rest. Each of these comparisons uses up one degree of freedom. The effects for interactions of pairs of factors (1st order interactions) are obtained from three two-way tables of means like that on p. 11 but in each case averaged over both levels of the third factor (Table 9B). The nitrogen and phosphorus interaction is thus:

$$\frac{[(NPK+NP)+(K+( ))]-[(NK+N)+(PK+P)]}{4} \quad (cf. \text{ 1.4 p.11})$$

These three interaction effects each take another degree of freedom. The last of the 7 degrees of freedom for treatment represents the 3-factor (2nd order) interaction, which is defined as half the difference in the interactions between any two factors at high and at low level of the third:

$$\frac{[(NPK+K)-(NK+PK)]-[(NP+( ))-(N+P)]}{4}$$

$$= \frac{(NPK+N+P+K)-(( )+PK+NP+NK)}{4}$$

The first form is given by the means of diagonals in two-way tables at high and low potassium respectively; the second, by the means of sets of 4 treatments at the corners of a cube-shaped 3-way table—lines joining these form two tetrahedra inscribed in the cube. The reader may like to draw this.

The sums of squares corresponding to these treatment effects may be found by the general method already given (p. 59); this can be applied to two-way tables of totals or means of any number of units but the sum of squares must be divided by the number of units in each total, or multiplied by that in each mean, to be obtained in terms of one unit; the sum of squares for the 3-factor interaction is obtained by subtraction. For 2^n experiments *only*, the sums of squares may be found from $(\text{effect})^2 N/4$ where N is the total number of units in the experiment. Thus if $\bar{x}_P$ is the mean for full phosphorus and $\bar{x}_p$ that for $\frac{1}{50}$ phosphorus, the sum of squares for phosphorus effect is

$$[(\bar{x}_P - \bar{x})^2 + (\bar{x}_p - \bar{x})^2]16 = \left[\frac{(\bar{x}_P - \bar{x}_p)}{2}\right]^2 2 \times 16 = \frac{(\bar{x}_P - \bar{x}_p)^2 32}{4}$$

With 1 degree of freedom for each treatment effect these are also variances and may be compared with the T × B interaction by the F test; or, which is equivalent, each 'effect' may be compared with zero by the *t* test (Table 9*B*). A significant interaction between, for example, nitrogen and phosphorus shows that the phosphorus effect on log weight differs according to the level of nitrogen; the *average* phosphorus effect is therefore of little interest, for we cannot maintain that we have tested phosphorus in a representative sample of the possible levels of nitrogen. The separate phosphorus effects at the different nitrogen levels, and *vice versa*, should therefore be discussed individually. By an extension of the same argument the nitrogen and phosphorus interaction would be of little interest if the three factor interaction were large and significant, and only the latter should then be discussed. On the other hand, if the interactions are found to be small and non-significant the mean effect of each factor, averaged over all levels of the others, is of more general application than in a simple experiment on one factor only.

Interaction diagrams. The first stage in examining the data from an experiment should be to plot appropriate diagrams. If these show nothing of interest, statistical analysis is likely to be waste of time; if they show interesting features these must be tested for significance and a preliminary idea of this can often be obtained, if no calculating machine is available, by inspection of diagrams plotted separately for each block.

The usual way of showing the effects of two factors in a factorial experiment is to plot yield y against level of one factor separately for each level of the other. If the curves are parallel there is no interaction, for the responses to the first factor are the same at each level of the second. This is seen in Fig. 3–2 (a), where in terms of log (dry weight) the effect of phosphorus at

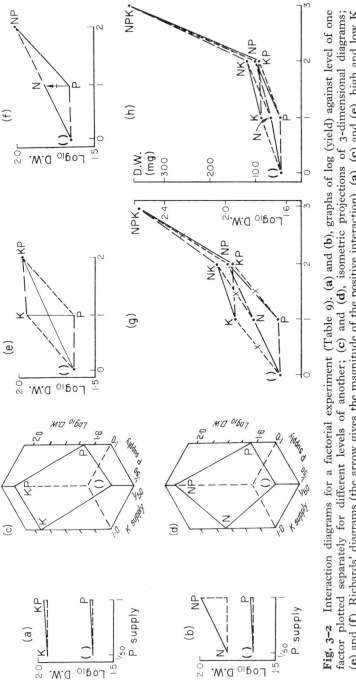

Fig. 3-2 Interaction diagrams for a factorial experiment (Table 9). (**a**) and (**b**), graphs of log (yield) against level of one factor plotted separately for different levels of another; (**c**) and (**d**), isometric projections of 3-dimensional diagrams; (**e**) and (**f**), Richards' diagrams (the arrow gives the magnitude of the positive interaction). (**a**), (**c**) and (**e**), high and low K and P (at low N) with almost no interaction; (**b**), (**d**) and (**f**), high and low N and P (at low K) with a positive interaction; (**g**) and (**h**), Richards' diagrams for the complete 2^3 factorial experiment, with a positive 3-factor interaction; (**g**) in terms of log (dry weight) and (**h**) in terms of dry weight.

high potassium is virtually the same as that at low potassium (both at low nitrogen), that is $(KP-K) \backsimeq (P-( ))$, and hence

$$\frac{(KP+( ))-(P+K)}{2} \backsimeq 0 \qquad (cf. \text{ 1.4 p.11})$$

This type of diagram is in fact a graphical two-way table. Fig. 3–2 (b) shows for phosphorus and nitrogen (both at low potassium) a positive interaction, for $(NP-N) > (P-( ))$ and therefore

$$\frac{(NP+( ))-(N+P)}{2} > 0$$

The diagrams in Figs. 3–2 (c) and (d) are isometric projections of 3-dimensional models, plotted on graph paper with a triangular grid; they show better the equal status of the two factors and that the interaction of for example nitrogen with phosphorus is the same as that of phosphorus with nitrogen.

The type of diagram in Figs. 3–2 (e) and (f), devised by F. J. RICHARDS (1941), shows the quantitative value as well as the form of the interaction and can moreover be extended to more than two factors (see below). The yields are plotted as ordinates as usual but the abscissae, instead of showing increments of one factor only, represent successive additions of any of the factors. At 0 is plotted the yield for the treatment with all factors (here two) at low level; '1' represents high dosage of a single factor but not of two simultaneously; '2' represents high dosage of two factors and with three factors '3' would represent all three at high level. If the quadrilateral formed is a parallelogram, interaction is absent; this is virtually true of Fig. 3–2 (e), where $(KP-K) \backsimeq (P-( ))$. However, it is obviously not so in Fig. 3–2 (f) and we can estimate the magnitude of the interaction effect as the distance between the mid-points of the two diagonals $(+0.07625)$; this is the difference of the means of the diagonals in the corresponding two way table.

The lack of interaction in terms of log (dry weight) shown by Fig. 3–2 (e) is consistent with a multiplicative type of interaction for the actual dry weights. If $(\log KP - \log K) = (\log P - \log ( ))$, then $KP/K = P/( )$ so that high phosphorus affects the dry weight in the same ratio with both low and high potassium; however, the phosphorus effect is so small that the interaction in terms of dry weight (Fig. 3–2 (h)) is also very small (p. 62).

Fig. 3–2 (g) shows a Richards' diagram for the complete 2^3 experiment. Note that different kinds of line are used for increments of the three nutrient elements. Each quadrilateral shows the interaction of two elements at a single level of the third; thus, ( ) N NP P shows the positive interaction of nitrogen and phosphorus at low potassium, while K NK NPK KP shows their larger positive interaction at high potassium. The mid-points of the potassium lines, marked x, give the means of high and low potassium for each combination of nitrogen and phosphorus; the quadrilateral formed by joining these therefore shows the two factor interaction between nitrogen and phosphorus averaged over high and low potassium. The other average two factor interactions could be found similarly. For each pair of factors there is a larger positive interaction at high level of the third than at low; this positive 2nd order interaction does not reach the conventional P0·05 level of significance but P is less than 0·1 and it is therefore worth considering. If real, it means that each element at high level fails to approach its full effect on growth unless both the others are also present at high level and it thus indicates the importance of nutrient balance.

The anti-log values of the treatment means (Table 9) are plotted in Fig. 3–2 (h) and the three factor interaction is seen to be considerably larger for the actual weights.

3.3.2   Factors at more than two levels

If possible, it is much better to use three levels of a factor than two, for we can then test whether the response is linear or curved and this provides another reason for covering a wide range (p. 65). Isometric projections of 3-dimensional diagrams (Figs. 3–2 (c) and (d)) are especially valuable, with many levels of each of two factors, for demonstrating the shape of the response surface (HEATH, 1969; HEATH and RUSSELL, 1954).

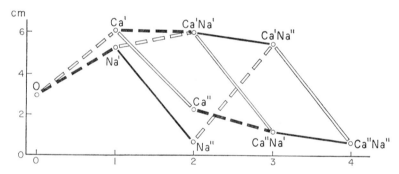

Fig. 3–3   Richards' diagram for 3^2 factorial experiment on growth of barley roots in water with o, 10^{-1} and $10^{-3}M$ Ca^{2+} and Na^+. Mean length of longest root (8 seedlings) after 14 days growth in darkness.

Fig. 3–3 shows a Richards' diagram for a 3×3 factorial experiment, carried out in class, to investigate effects of Ca^{2+} and Na^+ ions on root growth. Seedlings of barley were grown in darkness in distilled water with $CaCl_2$ and NaCl at concentrations of o·oooM, o·oo1M and o·1ooM in all nine combinations. These steps in concentration are treated formally as equal, which would be true on a log scale if the zero concentration had been o·oooo1M NaCl and $CaCl_2$. Length of the longest root was measured after 14 days' growth. There were four blocks, carried out by four pairs of students, with two plants per treatment in each. The diagram shows that compared with distilled water alone (shown as 0) 0·001M $CaCl_2$ (Ca′) was consistently beneficial and 0·1M $CaCl_2$ (Ca″) consistently harmful. These effects were almost independent of the level of NaCl: as long as some $CaCl_2$ was present there was practically no interaction and the two quadrilaterals concerned are almost parallelograms. 0·001M $CaCl_2$ or NaCl alone or together were beneficial, as compared with distilled water, and showed a large negative interaction; 0·1M NaCl (Na″) alone was very harmful but this effect was removed by 0·001M $CaCl_2$, as with Ringer's solution or sea water in many physiological experiments with animals. For plants, this and other experiments (F. J. Richards—personal communication) suggest that the presence of some Ca^{2+} is most important, Na^+ being inessential, and that pure distilled water can be very harmful.

3·4 Group or class experiments

In the Preface I have stated the belief that an understanding of science can only be gained by carrying out original investigation. By 'original' I do not mean investigation of a kind never before attempted, but that none of the people concerned (and this includes the master or lecturer in charge of a class) must have grounds for being at all sure of what the result will be—expecially they must not think they know the 'right' result. Only so can they savour the stimulus of discovery and only so come to realize that every experiment gives the 'right' answer to the question asked but the question is never a simple one and the interpretation of the answer never final. Investigations by single members of a class are unlikely, in the short periods usually available, to be on a large enough scale to yield significant results and much frustration lies behind the words at the end of innumerable project reports: '. . . but much further research will be needed before any conclusions can be drawn'. Moreover, no master or lecturer can adequately advise and assist in the design, execution and interpretation of a large number of individual investigations. Such advice and assistance are especially needed in the first year or two; learning by mistakes can be frustrating and is only of value if there is time to repeat the work correctly. In later years students should be able to carry out individual projects with much less supervision. The topics then chosen should have limited and specific objectives, and the choice of a suitable species is most important. At the University of Reading much of the practical work in horticulture (including whole plant physiology, entomology and plant pathology) is from the beginning in the form of original experiments carried out by the whole class. These are designed and organized by the staff in charge, to investigate problems in which they are personally interested and they therefore have the opportunity of communicating their interest; this cannot be done by remote control or by copying experiments out of a book; the class is in effect a research team with the member of staff as leader and he must devise the experiments himself in order to obtain the drive to organize a different course each year. This is arduous, but fortunately one experiment leads to another.

The simple schedule for these student experiments is as follows:

1. Each student (or pair of students if they have to work in pairs) should carry out *all* the treatments.

2. Each student (or pair) should carry out the treatments in a random order, determined afresh for each, either from tables of random numbers or, if there are only two treatments, by tossing a coin.

3. The boxes, pots or other units constituting the treatments carried out by one student (or pair) should be placed adjacent and arranged in a random order, which may be the same as that in which the treatments were carried out. Those carried out by different students (or pairs) may be widely separated if more convenient.

4. The experimental design is thus a randomized block layout, with position effects and student effects confounded as blocks.

5. Each box, pot or other unit *must* be labelled *at the time it is set up* with the treatment, date and student's initials. A plan should also be made.

6. Data may be collected as counts, measurements, weights or visual observations (preferably ranked on a numerical scale) as is most convenient in any particular experiment.

7. Each student must write up the experiment and in addition to recording his own data in detail, present the results from the other blocks together with the treatment means.

If such instructions are observed and numerical data are collected honestly and with due care, the results are available for statistical analysis at any time. They can make a real contribution to knowledge. It has been found advantageous for such experience of original investigation to precede by a year any formal instruction in statistics and design of experiments; these are by then seen to be necessary tools and a feeling for them has been acquired, together with an understanding of the meaning of variation.

The schedule relates to randomized blocks in space but if there is only one set, or a few sets, of apparatus for an investigation, students can be confounded with randomized blocks of time. Several investigations can be carried on in parallel in this way.

Many of the more horticultural experiments are of an empirical nature, to investigate questions of technique, and this is no great disadvantage for learning the principles of experimentation. Wide-ranging factorial experiments, if properly designed with a certain amount of imagination and carried out with technical competence, provide an almost infallible way to new and interesting findings.

Further reading

BAILEY, N. T. J. (1959). *Statistical Methods in Biology*. English Universities Press, London.

EDGE, E. (ed.) (1964). *Experiment. A Series of Scientific Case Histories*. British Broadcasting Corporation, London.

SAWYER, W. W. (1943). *Mathematician's Delight*. Penguin Books, Harmondsworth, Middlesex.

More advanced

COCHRAN, W. G. and COX, G. M. (1957). *Experimental Designs*. 2nd edn. Wiley, New York and London.

COX, D. R. (1958). *Planning of Experiments*. Wiley, New York and London.

FISHER, R. A. (1966). *The Design of Experiments*. 8th edn. Oliver and Boyd, Edinburgh and London.

YATES, F. (1937). *The Design and Analysis of Factorial Experiments*. Commonwealth Bureau of Soils, Farnham Royal, Bucks.

Tables

BARLOW, P. (1941). *Barlow's Tables of Squares, Cubes, Square Roots, etc.* (ed. L. J. Comrie) 4th edn. Spon. London.

FISHER, R. A. and YATES, F. (1963). *Statistical Tables for Biological, Agricultural and Medical Research*. 6th edn. Oliver and Boyd, Edinburgh and London.

LINDLEY, D. V. and MILLER, J. C. P. (1964). *Cambridge Elementary Statistical Tables*. Cambridge University Press, London.

References

AUDUS, L. J. (1959). *Plant Growth Substances*. 2nd edn. Leonard Hill, London.

BARTLETT, M. S. (1947). The use of transformations. *Biometrics*, **3**, 39–52.

BEER, G. de (1964). Mendel, Darwin and Fisher (1865–1965). *Notes Rec. R. Soc. Lond.* **19**, 192–226.

BLACKMAN, G. E. and RUTTER, A. J. (1946–50). Physiological and ecological studies in the analysis of plant environment. I–V. *Ann. Bot.*, **10**, 361–390; **11**, 125–158; **12**, 1–26; **13**, 453–489; **14**, 487–520.

COCHRAN, W. G. (1938). Some difficulties in the statistical analysis of replicated experiments. *Emp. J. exp. Agric.*, **6**, 157–175.

DARWIN, C. R. (1880). *The Power of Movement in Plants* (assisted by F. Darwin). John Murray, London.

DARWIN, C. R. (1958). *The autobiography of Charles Darwin, 1809–1882* (ed. N. Barlow). Collins, London.

EMDEN, H. F. van (1963). Observations on the effect of flowers on the activity of parasitic Hymenoptera. *Entomologist's mon. Mag.*, **98**, 265–270.

FISHER, R. A. (1963). *Statistical Methods for Research Workers*. 13th edn. Oliver and Boyd, Edinburgh and London.

HEATH, O. V. S. (1937). The growth in height and weight of the cotton plant under field conditions. *Ann. Bot.*, **1**, 515–520.

HEATH, O. V. S. (1943 a and b). Studies in the physiology of the onion plant I. An investigation of factors concerned in the flowering ('bolting') of onions grown from sets and its prevention. Parts 1 and 2. *Ann. appl. Biol.*, **30**, 208–220 and 308–319.

HEATH, O. V. S. (1950). Studies in stomatal behaviour V. The role of carbon dioxide in the light response of stomata Part I. *J. exp. Bot.*, **1**, 29–62.

HEATH, O. V. S. (1967). On the publication of the dates of experiments. *Inst. Biol. J.*, **14**, 140–143.

HEATH, O. V. S. (1969). *The Physiological Aspects of Photosynthesis.* Heinemann Educational Books, London and Stanford University Press, Stanford.

HEATH, O. V. S. and MATHUR, P. B. (1944). Studies in the physiology of the onion plant II. Inflorescence initiation and development. *Ann. appl. Biol.*, **31**, 173–186.

HEATH, O. V. S. and RUSSELL, J. (1954). Studies in stomatal behaviour VI. An investigation of the light responses of wheat stomata with the attempted elimination of control by the mesophyll. Part 2. *J. exp. Bot.*, **5**, 269–292.

HUDSON, J. P. (1957). The study of plant responses to soil moisture. In *Control of the Plant Environment*, ed. by J. P. Hudson, 113–127. Butterworths, London.

KERNER, A. von M. (1902). *The Natural History of Plants* (trans. F. W. Oliver). 2 vols. Blackie, London.

MENDEL, G. (1965). *Experiments in Plant Hybridisation* (with commentary by R. A. Fisher). Oliver and Boyd, Edinburgh and London.

OBEID, M., MACHIN, D. and HARPER, J. L. (1967). Influence of density on plant to plant variation in fibre flax, *Linum usitatissimum. Crop Sci.*, **7**, 471–3.

PFEFFER, W. F. P. (1900–3). *The Physiology of Plants.* (trans. A. J. Ewart) 3 vols. Clarendon Press, Oxford.

POINCARÉ, H. (1914). *Science and Method.* (trans. F. Maitland) Nelson, London.

RICHARDS, F. J. (1934). On the use of simultaneous observations on successive leaves for the study of physiological change in relation to leaf age. *Ann. Bot.*, **48**, 497–503.

RICHARDS, F. J. (1941). The diagrammatic representation of the results of physiological and other experiments designed factorially. *Ann. Bot.*, **5**, 249–261.

SACHS, J. von (1887). *Lectures on the Physiology of Plants.* (trans. H. Marshall Ward). Clarendon Press, Oxford.

SKENE, MacGREGOR (1924). *The Biology of Flowering Plants.* Sidgwick and Jackson, London.

SALISBURY, E. J. (1961). *Weeds and Aliens.* Collins, London.

SALISBURY, E. J. (1967). The reproduction and germination of *Limosella aquatica. Ann. Bot.*, **31**, 147–162.

WALLIS, G. (1926). *The Art of Thought.* Jonathan Cape, London and Toronto.

Date Due

AUG 13 2009			